The White River Ute War
Colorado, 1879

The White River Ute War Colorado, 1879

The Ute War: A History of the White River Massacre

Thomas F. Dawson and F. J. V. Skiff

Besieged By the Utes: The Massacre of 1879

E. V. Sumner

The Ute War of 1879

Thomas Sturgis

LEONAUR

The White River Ute War Colorado, 1879
The Ute War: A History of the White River Massacre
by Thomas F. Dawson and F. J.V. Skiff
Besieged By the Utes: The Massacre of 1879
by E.V. Sumner
The Ute War of 1879
by Thomas Sturgis

FIRST EDITION

First published under the titles
The Ute War: A History of the White River Massacre
Besieged By the Utes: The Massacre of 1879
The Ute War of 1879

Leonaur is an imprint of Oakpast Ltd
Copyright in this form © 2014 Oakpast Ltd

ISBN: 978-1-78282-273-8 (hardcover)
ISBN: 978-1-78282-274-5 (softcover)

http://www.leonaur.com

Publisher's Notes

The views expressed in this book are not necessarily
those of the publisher.

Contents

The Ute War: A History of the White River Massacre

Contents

Introduction

In giving this little book to the public, no effort is made at literary excellence. The one aim of the book is to furnish in connected and comprehensive shape an account of the recent uprising of the Utes, and the origin and attending circumstances of the entire trouble from the time of Johnson's attack upon Agent Meeker, including the Thornburgh fight at Milk River, the agency massacre, the captivity of the women, and other incidents of interest. The authors feel competent to assume this task. They have, as editors of the *Tribune*, written a complete history of the affair from day to day, and need simply to put in book form what they have heretofore published. We have culled largely from the Denver Tribune and other papers, including the New York *Herald* and the Chicago *Tribune*, in preparing the book, and have added some information never before given to the world. In submitting this work to the public we desire simply to say that it is reliable. No facts have been either suppressed or exaggerated for sensational effect.

JOSIE MEEKER.

Chapter 1

The Thornburgh Massacre

It was about noon on the 1st day of October of the present year, (1879), that the first news of the Milk River fight between the United States troops under Major T. T. Thornburgh and the Ute Indians, reached Denver and the remaining portions of the outside world. For, although the battle had occurred two days previous to this time, the long distance between the scene of the conflict and a telegraph station, and the rough mountain trail lined, it was supposed, with Indians, had prevented any earlier communication of the news. The first information of the disaster came in the shape of a telegraphic dispatch, dated at Laramie City, Wyoming, and was sent by Col. Stephen W. Downey, delegate to Congress from Wyoming, to Governor Pitkin. It was as follows:

Laramie City, October 1, 1879.

To Governor Pitkin, Denver:

The White River Utes have met Colonel Thornburgh's command, sent to quell disturbances at the agency, killing Thornburgh himself, and killing and wounding many of his officers, men and horses, whereby the safety of the whole command is imperilled. I shall warn our people in the North Park, and trust that you will take such prompt action as will protect your people and result in giving the War Department control of the savages, in order to protect the settlers from massacres, provoked by the present temporising policy of the government with reference to Indian affairs, in all time to come.

Stephen W. Downey.

Numerous dispatches followed the one given above, and the news spread from lip to ear, until by two o'clock the entire population of the city was excited to an unusual pitch. The reports were mainly vague and unsatisfactory, and imagination assisted greatly to swell the volume of horror and the prospect of war and murder on our own frontier. To relate half the stories that fancy wove into shape and fluent lips spoke into open ears in that one afternoon would be to fill this volume, and to impart to it the character of romance which it is not intended to give it. For several weeks there had been talk in the newspapers about trouble with the Utes, and the public at large had been informed of the savage treatment received by Agent Meeker at White River at the hands of the Indians; but the masses had passed these warnings by quite heedlessly, and many had doubtless forgotten that there had ever been any cause for alarm. During the few days previous the newspapers themselves had ceased in a degree to speak of affairs on the reservation. The soldiers under Major Thornburgh having been sent out from Fort Steele, all seemed to feel a sense of security on behalf of the people at the agency. It was tacitly agreed that the sending in of the troops had put an end to demonstrations on the part of the Indians.

This was the quiet before the storm—the calm, clear morning before the dark and storming afternoon. The surprise was complete. Had the troops marched into the ambush laid for them at Milk River and been suddenly fired upon before seeing an Indian, their astonishment could have been but a degree greater than that felt by the people of Colorado and Wyoming on receiving the news. To use a favourite and expressive phrase of the reportorial brotherhood, it *fell like a bolt of lightning from a clear sky.*

Many days passed before any definite information could be obtained, and during that interim the wires were fairly humming with anxious inquiries for friends in Colorado from all parts of the globe, from news papers and from the government authorities, and the responses to all, many of which embodied the startling rumours which were floating in the atmosphere and passing from one person to another, in lieu of something more authoritative to send.

The uncertainty in regard to the whereabouts of the Indians and the certainty in regard to their commit ting depredations wherever an opportunity might offer, were causes for the most serious apprehension in be half of the prospectors, miners and stock raisers along the line of the reservation. Governor Pitkin took immediate steps to inform the frontiersmen of the danger to which they were subjected. He sent or caused to be sent couriers to North Park, Middle Park,

Bear River, Snake River, Grand River, Eagle River, Gunnison River and its tributaries, Coal Creek, Ohio Creek, Anthracite Creek, Taylor River, etc.; Lake City, Silverton, Ouray, Rico, Animas City, and other points which it was believed would be in danger in case the Indians should scatter or determine to attack the settlements. Militia companies were organised and drilled, and arms and ammunition distributed by the State as fast as they could be obtained from the government. In less time than a week the entire State was in arms, and was well ready to fight the Indians before further news was received from Milk River.

CHAPTER 2

Origin of the Trouble With the Utes

While we are anxiously awaiting this intelligence, it will certainly not be out of place to revert briefly to the circumstances which immediately preceded and led up to the Thornburgh affair.

The origin of the difficulties with the Utes seems to have lain partially in the fact that this tribe, like the Cheyennes, could not content themselves upon their reservation. The country north of the Colorado Reservation is very desirable for farming and grazing purposes, and is thickly settled. For three or four years past the Indians have been in the habit of intruding into this district, as well as into North and Middle Parks, which practice has caused considerable annoyance to settlers, particularly on Snake, Bear and Grand Rivers. There are many lawless persons in the vicinity, it is said, who for years have carried on a brisk trade with the Indians, supplying them with whisky and ammunition, causing constant complaints to the Indian Office.

Depredations have also been committed by the Indians along the valleys of the rivers referred to. In the fall of 1877 Agent Danforth visited that country, together with Lieutenant Parke, of the Ninth Cavalry, United States Army, with a view to the adoption of measures to protect the settlers and break up this unlawful traffic. They reported in September, 1877, that it would be necessary to establish a military post there, that this would keep the Indians on their reservation, serve to protect the settlers and break up the unlawful trade referred to. The recommendation was never complied with.

It was about this time that Hon. N. C. Meeker was appointed by President Hayes agent at White River. He found affairs in a deplorable state. Many of the Indians had left the reservation, and had gone as far north as Sweetwater Creek in Wyoming, Chief Douglass being among those who had wandered from the flock. Great dissatisfaction existed because of ill treatment by former agents, and there was no little talk of war. But Agent Meeker soon succeeded in restoring quiet among the discontented, and soon again all went well.

Very soon after establishing himself at the agency Mr. Meeker commenced to introduce some reforms into the system of conducting Indian Agencies, in which efforts he had the co-operation of the government. It was a pet theory with him that he could make the agency self-supporting by stock raising and agriculture, and that, by an effort in the proper direction, the Indians could be educated. He did not believe in wasting time on the old Indians of fixed customs, but thought that the young might be induced to attend school and grow up educated in the English language and trained in the manners of civilized society. For the accomplishment of the latter purpose he took his daughter, Miss Josephine Meeker, the heroine of this narrative, with him to the agency, and she established a school for the benefit of the Indian juveniles. The agency was removed during Mr. Meeker's administration twenty miles from White River, from the old site, to Powell's Bottom, one of the best favoured and most beautiful tracts of land on the continent. Here he began his agricultural demonstrations, which were the direct cause—at least the principal one assigned by the Indians—for their outbreak and murder of the agent.

The Indian trouble was really brewing all summer. In June the Utes began burning the forests and grasses along the line of their reservation, a distance of over three hundred miles. Roving bands wandered up and down the entire country, leaving a trail of fire wherever they went. Fires were started in uninhabited districts at first, but in August the houses of Major Thompson and a Mr. Smart on Bear River, Routt County, were burned by Indians who were seen and recognised. Complaints for arson were sworn out before Judge Beck, First Judicial District, who issued warrants for the arrest of two Indians named Bennett and Chinaman.

Sheriff Bessey and a posse followed the Indians into the reservation to execute the warrants, but they were unable to find the criminals. Chief Douglass denied the right to arrest Indians on a reservation. This fact was officially reported to Governor Pitkin by Judge Beck, and he applied to General Pope for troops to execute the warrants, on the ground that no Indian guilty of arson could escape punishment for crimes by taking refuge on the reservation. General Pope at once ordered a company of cavalry, then scouting in Middle Park, to the agency to arrest the Indians or assist the sheriff.

Meanwhile Father Meeker, the White River Agent, had difficulty with certain members of the tribe and had been rudely handled by Johnson, a leading chief. A ploughman was also shot at and exciting scenes ensued.

As these were the events which led to the following more serious incidents, we reproduce entire Mr. Meeker's own explanation of the difficulty, which was that which follows:

Having finished the ploughing of one field we started on another. This field was one of about 200 acres, not yet fenced, but only half was to be ploughed, the remainder was to be irrigated for a hay meadow. Since so many Indian horses eat up the natural hay, we have to go from four to seven miles to cut hay, and even there the horses leave only a part. A chief object in moving the agency was to obtain tillable land, and this particular tract of 200 acres was an inducement. But after we had irrigated a bed 100 feet wide and half a mile long several Indians objected and Jane in particular. Her man Parviets had built a corral on the ground, though he was told previously that the land would be ploughed; and Antelope was another. Both of these had been off in Middle Park, cutting up generally, and they had to be sent for and brought back, and when they came fire followed them all the way back to Bear River.

The claim that Jane and Antelope made was that this is the Utes' country; that they had fixed themselves and did not want to move, for the grass was good and they wanted it all the while for their horses. Being close to the agency, for the buildings are on the lot, it was handy and they wanted it. Besides, they said the Utes did not want any more land ploughed, there was enough now, and they wanted to live just as they had lived. Jane was told that there were plenty of places just as good; that the *employés* would move everything without any trouble to her, and make things enough sight better; and she was told, too, that if the buildings were moved she would be sure to follow and claim land close by, and so the agent could have no chance to plough at all. She said he might plough off in another place, and she indicated, as Douglass and others did afterward, that a certain tract, covered with grease wood, cut up with sloughs, and white with alkali, was good to plough, though it would take three months to clear the surface.

18

No, she would listen to nothing; that piece of land was to be theirs, and they wouldn't have it ploughed, for they had taken it, which was something like the case when Greeley was first settled, when men wanted to locate their share on 160 acres next to the town centre. Therefore the ploughs were ordered to run, but before a single round had been ploughed, there came two Indians with guns and forbid the ploughing. When the ploughman came back he reported to the Agent, who told him to go ahead. And so the sulky-breaker went ahead, and for an hour or so peace seemed restored; but after awhile the ploughman reported that he was shot at from a little bunch of sage brush, where two Indians were seen lying, and the ball whistled close to his person. Of course ploughing was ordered stopped and the team turned out. Then Douglass was sent for, but he would do nothing. This was the Utes' country, and they wanted it for their horses.

Then Jack, the chieftain, a rival to Douglass, was sent for, ten miles up the river. Jack has a big body of big Indians under him, and it was scarcely two hours before as many as twenty of them, with Jack at their head, came down on the full run, for Jack had been told that the agent was going to telegraph to Washington, but before he did so he wanted to know whether all the Utes united to stop the ploughing, and all of them should be heard. "Then followed a talk lasting nearly to sundown, when it was decided that the agent might plough that bed, but no more. The agent said that would not do at all. Then it was decided that he might plough more and have it all, so the thing seemed settled. However, it was not settled.

The next day the plough started, but it had not gone half around before out came Parviets and Antelope and threatened dire vengeance if any more than that land was ploughed, which, by the way, was a fine piece to fence, being in all about six acres, and requiring more fencing than a square of one hundred acres. Still, the plough ran an hour or so, doing first-rate work. But by this time the *employés* began to think there was likely to be different kind of work to do than they came hither for, and so the ploughman was ordered to retreat from the enemy. About this time the remark was made to George, 'This is getting rather interesting,' to which he replied, 'It may be to you, but I can't see it for my part.'

Then Jack was sent for again, and he came down with a big lot of retainers, earlier than the day before, and a big long talk was had. The agent sat for hours in a hot room filled with tobacco smoke, and listened to speeches of which he understood nothing, and during all the time he said nothing—silently representing the Government of the United States.

Among the speeches was one by Douglass, which was the closing plea, or summing of the case, lasting nearly half an hour, and then it was understood why Douglass was made chief that is, on account of his eloquence. First, he spoke in poetic Ute, not in the ordinary vernacular. Second, the words were uttered with perfect distinctness, and yet quite rapidly. Third, the sentences were measured. There would be three sentences of about fifteen words each; then a sentence of thirty or forty words, and so on. The Indians listened to him with the utmost attention, and some seemed to shed the sympathetic tear, for frequently in his gestures he seemed to embrace some object, and with fervour and love. It was afterward learned that he spoke of the unity of all the Indian tribes, the Utes, the Bannocks, Arapahoes, Cheyennes, Pawnees, Apaches and Navajos, and then of the fatherly care of the government, embracing and caring for all as if they were the children of one father.

Soon after the conclusion of the speech, Douglass asked the agent what he would do for Jane if she would move off. The reply was that he would move the corral, help her husband build a log house, dig a well, give them a stove, and have everything nice. This was agreed to, and the agent was allowed to have the land. The impression is, that if the Indians had been free to choose, they would have forbidden an other furrow to be turned.

Colonel John W. Steele, an agent of the post office department, visited White River Agency immediately after this occurrence. Colonel Steele, speaking of the scenes and incidents of his visit, which fell on the 12th of September, says:

I soon learned that the agent, Mr. Meeker, had, a short time before my arrival, been violently assaulted by a Ute chief named Johnson, and severely, if not dangerously, injured. The white labourers told me that they had been fired on while ploughing in the field and driven to the agency buildings, but that they were not much scared, as they thought the Indians only wanted to prevent the work and fired to frighten them. Finding Mr. W. H. Post, the agent's chief clerk and postmaster, at White River in his office, I proceeded to transact my business with him. While engaged at this the Indians began to congregate in the building. Mr. Post introduced me to Chiefs Ute Jack, Washington, Antelope and others. Ute Jack seemed to be the leader, and asked me my name and business. I told him. He inquired if I came from Fort Steele and if the soldiers were coming. I replied that I knew nothing of the soldiers.

Jack said: 'No 'fraid of soldiers. Fort Steele soldiers no fight. Utes heap fight.'

He again asked me my name and when I was going away. I replied: 'In the morning.'

Jack said: 'Better go quick.'

I offered him a cigar and repeated that I would go in the morning. He then inquired for Mr. Meeker, and said to Post: 'Utes heap talk to me. Utes say agent plough no more. Utes say Meeker must go 'way. Meeker say Utes work. Work! work! Ute no like work. Ute no work. Ute no school; no like school,' and much more of the same sort.

Jack asked Mr. Post when the Indian goods would be issued. Post replied: 'In two moons.' Jack said the goods were issued at the Uncompahgre Agency; that four Indians had come from there and told him.

Post replied: 'Guess not.'

Mr. Post said to me: 'Every fall there is more or less discontent among the Indians, which finally dies out. This year there is more than usual. Jack's band got mad last week because I would not issue rations to some Uintah Utes who had come here, and all the bucks refused to draw their supplies. The squaws drew for themselves and children.'

Mr. Meeker came in for a short time while we were talking. About 8 o'clock I went to his quarters, and found him propped up in his armchair with pillows, evidently suffering severely from injuries received from the assault of Chief Johnson. After a short talk we discovered that we had formerly been fellow townsmen, which opened the way for a free conversation about mutual acquaintances. After which Mr. Meeker said: 'I came to this agency in the full belief that I could civilize these Utes;

that I could teach them to work and become self-supporting. I thought that I could establish schools and interest both Indians and their children in learning. I have given my best efforts to this end, always treating them kindly but firmly. They have eaten at my table, and received continued kindness from my wife and daughter and all the *employés* about the agency.

Their complaints have been heard patiently and all reasonable requests have been granted them, and now the man for whom I have done the most—for whom I have built the only Indian house on the reservation, and who has frequently eaten at my table—has turned on me without the slightest provocation, and would have killed me but for the white labourers who got me away. No Indian raised his hand to prevent the out rage, and those who had received continued kindness from myself and family stood around and laughed at the brutal assault. They are an unreliable and treacherous race.'

Mr. Meeker further said that previous to this assault on him he had expected to see the discontent die out, as soon as the annuity goods arrived, but he was now anxious about the matter. In reply to an inquiry, he said that the whole complaint of the Indians was against ploughing the land, against work and the school. I told him I, thought there was great danger of an outbreak, and I thought that he should leave the agency at once. To this he made no reply.

Shortly after, Ute Jack came into the room where we were sitting, and proceeded to catechise me nearly as before. He then turned to Mr. Meeker and repeated the talk about work, and then asked the agent if he had sent for soldiers. Mr. Meeker told him he had not. Jack then said: 'Utes have heap more talk.'

During the conversation Mr. Meeker said that Chief Douglass was head chief at that agency, but that he had no followers and little influence. That Douglass and his party had remained on the reservation all the summer and had been friendly to the whites; that Colorow, Ute Jack, Johnson and their followers paid no attention to his orders and had been off the reservation most of the summer; that Chief Ouray was head chief, but had lost his influence with and control of the northern Utes.

I again urged on him the danger of remaining at the agency, when he told me he would send for troops for protection. During this conversation the Indians had remained around the agency buildings, making much noise. About ten o'clock I went to the quarters assigned me for the night in the store-house office. Soon after this the Indians began shouting and dancing in one of the agency buildings and around the agent's quarters. About midnight Mr. Meeker attempted to quiet them, but was only partially successful, and the red devils made it exceedingly uncomfortable for me most of the night. I was told in the morning that the Indians had had a war dance. Those who saw and could have described the scene are all dead now. At daylight the bucks had all disappeared. After breakfast I called on Mr. Meeker in his room to bid him goodbye. He told me he had written for troops, and requested me to telegraph for relief as soon as I reached Rawlins.

It was immediately after this occurrence that Mr. Meeker applied to Governor Pitkin for troops for protection, and he made a request of General Pope, who at once ordered Major Thornburgh on the mission in which he met his unfortunate death. General Pope issued orders, September 19th, for four companies of cavalry to concentrate at White River Agency. Two of these companies were ordered from Fort Fred. Steele, one from Fort Saunders and one from Pagosa Springs. The latter company was a negro command, and had been skirting along the western boundary of the reservation. It was ordered north two months previous, in response to the governor's telegram relative to the Indians firing the forests.

CHAPTER 3

The March of Thornburgh's Command

Major T. T. Thornburgh, commanding officer of the Fourth United States Infantry, and for the past year in command at Fort Fred. Steele on the Union Pacific Railroad in Wyoming, was placed in charge of the expedition, which left Rawlins for White River Agency, September 24. The command consisted of two companies, D and F of the Fifth Cavalry, Company E of the Third Cavalry, and Company E of the Fourth Infantry, the officers included in the detachment being Captains Payne and Lawson of the Fifth Cavalry, Lieutenant Paddock of the Third Cavalry, and Lieutenants Price and Wooley of the Fourth Infantry, with Dr. Grimes accompanying the command as surgeon. Following the troops was a supply train of thirty-three wagons.

When the command reached the place known as Old Fortification Camp, Company E of the Fourth Infantry, with Lieutenant Price in command, was dropped from the command, the design of this step being to afford protection to passing supply trains, and to act as a reserve in case there was demand for it.

Major Thornburgh turned his force towards the Indian country in deep earnest, with the balance of his command consisting of the three cavalry companies numbering about 160 men.

Having been directed to use all dispatch in reaching the agency, the major marched forward with as great rapidity as possible. The route selected is not well travelled and is mountainous, and of course the troops did not proceed so rapidly as they might have done on more familiar highways.

Nothing was seen of or heard from the Indians until Bear River, which runs north of the reservation and almost parallel with the northern line, was reached. At the crossing of this stream, about sixty-five miles from White River Agency, ten Indians, headed by two Ute chiefs, Colorow and Jack, made their appearance. They were closely questioned, but professed great friendliness for the whites and would betray none of the secrets of their tribe. They declared that they were merely out on a hunt, and repeated that they were friends of the white man and of the Great Father's government, and especially of the Great Father's soldiers.

After this parley, which took place September 26, Thornburgh sent his last telegram from camp:

> Have met some of the Ute chiefs here. They seem friendly and promise to go with me to the agency. They say the Utes don't understand why we come here. I have tried to explain satisfactorily; don't now anticipate trouble.

The conclusion is that Thornburgh was one of the most prudent and discreet of officers, but that he was thrown off his guard by the savages.

The march was continued and nothing more was seen of the Indians, though a close watch by keen-eyed scouts was kept up for them, until William's Fork, a small tributary of Bear River, was reached, when the same ten Indians first seen again quite suddenly and very mysteriously appeared. They renewed their protestations of friendship, while they covertly and critically eyed the proportions of the command. They made a proposition to the commander that he take an escort of five soldiers and accompany them to the agency. A halt was called and Major Thornburgh summoned his staff to a consultation. After carefully discussing the matter with a due regard for the importance, the advantage and disadvantage of the step, the officers' council came to the conclusion that it was not wise to accept this proffer on the part of the Indians, as it might lead to another Modoc trap, and to Thornburgh's becoming another Canby. Thornburgh's scout, Mr. Joseph Rankin, was especially strong in opposition to the request of the Indians.

Major Thornburgh then concluded to march his column within hailing distance of the agency, where he would accept the proposition of the Indians.

But he was never allowed to carry out his designs. Here it became apparent how thin the disguise of friendship had been, and Thornburgh was soon convinced how fatal would have been the attempt for him, accompanied by only five men, to treat with them.

The command had reached the point where the road crosses Milk River, another tributary of the Bear, inside the reservation and in the limits of Summit County, about twenty-five miles north of the agency, when they were attacked by the hostiles, numbering, it is believed, between two hundred and fifty and three hundred warriors, who had been lying in ambush.

The scene of the attack was peculiarly fitted for the Indian method of warfare. When Thornburgh's command entered the ravine or *cañon* they found themselves between two bluffs 1,300 yards apart. Those on the south 100 feet. The road to the agency ran through the ravine in a south-easterly direction, following the bend of the Milk River, at a distance of 500 yards. Milk River is a narrow, shallow stream, which here flows in a south-westerly direction through a narrow *cañon*. Through this *cañon*, after making a detour to avoid some very difficult ground, the wagon road passes for three or four miles. Along the stream is a growth of cottonwood trees; but its great advantage as an ambuscade lies in the narrowness of the *cañon*. On the top of the two ranges of bluffs the Indians had in trenched themselves in a series of pits, so that when the troops halted at the first volley, they stood between two fires at a range of only 650 yards from either bluff.

The battle took place on the morning of September 29. The locality of the ambush had been known as Bad Cañon, but it will hereafter be described as Thornburgh's Pass.

Lieutenant Cherry discovered the ambush and was ordered by Major Thornburgh to hail the Indians. He took fifteen men of "E" Company for this work. Major Thornburgh's orders were not to make the first fire on the Indians, but to await an attack from them. After the Indians and Cherry's hailing party had faced each other for about ten minutes, Mr. Rankin, the scout, who is an old Indian fighter, seeing the danger in which the command was placed, hurried direct to Major Thornburgh's side and requested him to open fire on the enemy, saying at the same time that that was their only hope.

Major Thornburgh replied:

"My God! I dare not; my orders are positive, and if I violate them and survive, a court martial and ignominious dismissal may follow. I feel as though myself and men were to be murdered."

Major Thornburgh, with Captain Payne, was riding at the head of the column, Company "F," Fifth Cavalry, in advance, Lieutenant Lawson commanding next, and "D" Company, Fifth Cavalry, Lieutenant

Paddock commanding, about a mile and a half to the rear, in charge of the wagon train.

Cherry had moved out at a gallop with his men from the right flank, and noticed a like movement of about twenty Indians from the left of the Indians' position. He approached to within a couple hundred yards of the Indians and took off his hat and waved it, but the response was a shot fired at him, wounding a man of the party and killing his horse. This was the first shot, and was instantly followed by a volley from the Indians. The work had now begun in real earnest, and seeing the advantage of the position he then held, Cherry dismounted his detachment and deployed along the crest of the hill to prevent the Indians flanking his position, or to cover his retreat if found necessary to retire upon the wagon train, which was then coming up slowly, guarded by Lieutenant Paddock's company, D, Fifth cavalry.

Orders were sent to pack the wagons and cover them, with the company guarding them. The two companies in advance were Captain Payne's company, F, Fifth cavalry, and Lieutenant Lawson's company, E, Third cavalry, which were dismounted and deployed as skirmishers, Captain Payne on the left and Lieutenant Lawson on the right.

From Cherry's position he could see that the Indians were trying to cut him off from the wagons, and at once sent word to Major Thornburgh, who then withdrew the line slowly, keeping the Indians in check until opposite the point which his men had, when, seeing that the Indians were concentrating to cut off his retreat, Captain Payne, with Company F, Fifth cavalry, was ordered to charge the hill, which he did in gallant style, his horse being shot under him and several of his men wounded.

The Indians being driven from this point, the company was rallied on the wagon train. Major Thornburgh then gave orders to Cherry to hold his position and cover Lieutenant Lawson's retreat, who was ordered to fall back slowly with the company horses of his company.

Cherry called for volunteers of twenty men, who responded promptly and fought with desperation. Nearly every man was wounded before he reached camp, and two men were killed. Cherry brought every wounded man in with him.

Lieutenant Lawson displayed the greatest coolness and courage during this retreat, sending up ammunition to Cherry's men when once they were nearly without it.

Simultaneously with the attack on Thornburgh's advance the Indians swept in between the troops and the wagon train, which was

MAJOR T. T. THORNBURGH

protected by D Company, Lieutenant Paddock commanding. The desperate situation of the soldiers in the ravine was at once apparent to every officer and man in the ambush. The soldiers fought valiantly, desperately and the Indians shrank under the terrible counter fire. A more complete trap could not be contrived, for the troops were not only outnumbered but exposed to a galling fire from bluffs over the edge of which it was impossible to reach the foe, as the range of sight would, of course, carry bullets clear over the Indian pits.

Major Thornburgh was here and there and every where directing the attack, the defence and later the retreat. He was constantly exposed to fire and the wonder is that his intrepidity did not win his death ere it did. Captain Payne and his company under orders from Thornburgh fell back to a knoll followed by Lieutenant Lawson and company, the retreat being covered by Lieutenant Cherry's command. Hemmed in at both outlets of the pass and subjected to a steady deathly fire from the heights on either side, the troops were melting down under the savage massacre.

Major Thornburgh, seeing the terrible danger in which his command was placed from the position of the Indians, at once mounted about twenty men, and at the head of them he dashed forward with a valour, and made a charge on the savages between the command and the train.

It was in this valorous dash that Thornburgh met his fate, thirteen of his bold followers also being killed, the gallant leader falling within four hundred yards of the wagons.

The remainder of the command then in retreat for the train corral, followed the path led by Thornburgh and his men. As Captain Payne's company was about to start, or had started, his saddle girth broke and he got a fearful fall. One of his men dismounted and assisted him on his horse, the captain's horse having run away. F Company, Fifth, followed by the captain, he being badly bruised, reached the wagon train to find it being packed, and Lieutenant Paddock fighting the Indians, and wounded. Lieutenants Lawson and Cherry fell back slowly with their companies dismounted and fighting all the way, every man doing his duty.

The stubborn resistance of Lieutenant Cherry in covering the retreat gave time for the troops at the train to form temporary breastworks of men's bundles, flour, sacks of corn, wagons and dead horses, and when the last detachment had reached the Paddock corral the soldiers fought and entrenched, horses being shot down rapidly and the foe settling into position on all the high points about them. Captain Payne, who by Thornburgh's death came into command, drew up eight of the wagons and ranged them as a sort of a breastwork along the northern and eastern sides of an oval, at the same time cutting transverse trenches on the western and southern points of the oval, along the line of which the men "posted themselves.

Inside the oval eight more wagons were drawn up for the purpose of corralling the animals, and there was also a pit provided for sheltering the wounded. Behind the pits ran a path to the nearest bend of Milk River, which was used for obtaining water. The command held their position until 8:30 o'clock that night, when the Indians withdrew.

In the engagement there were twelve soldiers killed and forty-two wounded. Every officer in the command was shot with the exception of Lieutenant Cherry, of the Fifth Cavalry. The Indians killed from one hundred and fifty to two hundred mules be longing to the government. Surgeon Grimes was wounded but was able for duty. The troops had about six days' supplies.

When the roll was called, as the darkness of night settled about the beleaguered troops, it was found that the following men had been killed or wounded in the battle:

Killed.

Major Thornburgh, Fourth Infantry.
First Sergeant John Dolan, Company. F, Fifth Cavalry.
Private John Burns, Company F, Fifth Cavalry.
Michael Fieretom, Company F, Fifth Cavalry.
Amos D. Miller, Company F, Fifth Cavalry.
Samuel McKee, Company F, Fifth Cavalry.
Thomas Mooney, Company D, Fifth Cavalry.
Michael Lynch, Company D, Fifth Cavalry.
Charles Wright, Company D, Fifth Cavalry.
Dominick Caff, Company E, Third Cavalry.
Wagonmaster McKinsley.
Teamster McGuire.

Wounded.

Captain Payne, Fifth Cavalry, slight wound in the arm and side.
Lieutenant Paddock, Fifth Cavalry, flesh wound in the hip.
Dr. Grimes, flesh wound in the shoulder.
Sergeant John Merrill, Company F, Fifth Cavalry.

Trumpeter Frederick Sutcliff, Company F, Fifth Cavalry.
Trumpeter John McDonald, Company F, Fifth Cavalry.
Private Just, Company F, Fifth Cavalry.
Private Gibbs, Company F, Fifth Cavalry.
Private John Hoaxey, Company F, Fifth Cavalry.
Private Emil Kurzman, Company F, Fifth Cavalry.
Private Eugene Patterson, Company F, Fifth Cavalry.
Private Frank Simmons, Company F, Fifth Cavalry.
Private Eugene Shiek, Company F, Fifth Cavalry.
Private Edouz, Company F, Fifth Cavalry.
Private William Eizer, Company F, Fifth Cavalry.
Private Gattlied, Company F, Fifth Cavalry.
Private Steiger, Company F, Fifth Cavalry.
Private Nicholas, Company D, Fifth Cavalry.
Private Heeney, Company D, Fifth Cavalry.
Private Thomas, Company D, Fifth Cavalry.
Private Lynch, Company D, Fifth Cavalry.
Private Frederick. Bernhard, Company D, Fifth Cavalry.
Private E. Muller, Company D, Fifth Cavalry.
Sergeant James Montgomery, Company E, Third Cavalry.
Sergeant Allen Lupton, Company E, Third Cavalry.
Corporal C. F. Eichmurtzel, Company E, Third Cavalry.
Frank Hunter, Company E, Third Cavalry.
Private James Conway, Company E, Third Cavalry.
Private John Crowley, Company E, Third Cavalry.
Private W. H. Clark, Company E, Third Cavalry.
Private Orlando Durand, Company E, Third Cavalry.
Private Thomas Ferguson, Company E, Third Cavalry.
Private Thomas Lewis, Company E, Third Cavalry.
Private Edward Lavelle, Company E, Third Cavalry.
Private Willard Mitchell, Company E, Third Cavalry.
Private John Mahoney, Company E, Third Cavalry.
Private James Patterson, Company E, Third Cavalry.
Private W. M. Schubert, Company E, Third Cavalry.
Private Thomas McNamara, Company E, Third Cavalry.
Private Marcus Hanson, Company E, Third Cavalry.
Private James Budha, Company E, Third Cavalry.
Private James Donovan, Company E, Third Cavalry.

In the fight twenty-three Indians were killed and two severely wounded, how many slightly wounded is not known. Among the Indians killed were Ouray's nephew, Wattsconavot (meaning Doctor), and Catolowop (meaning Fat Man).

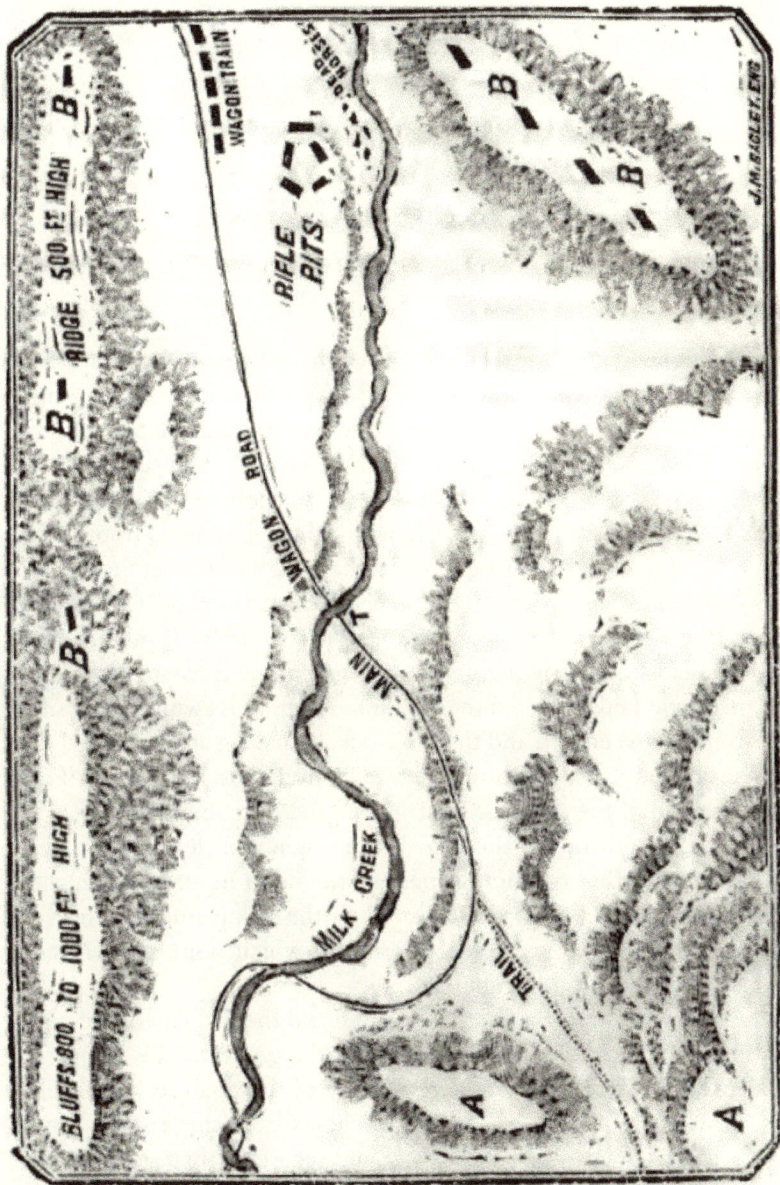

BLUFFS 800 TO 1000 FT HIGH

B — RIDGE 500 FT HIGH — B

B — B —

WAGON TRAIN

DEAD HORSES

B

B

RIFLE PITS

WAGON ROAD

MAIN

MILK CREEK

TRAIL

A

A

J.M.BIGLER.ENG

CHAPTER 4

The Six Days' Siege

During the early part of the first night of the siege under cover of the darkness, while the Indians had temporarily ceased their murderous vigil, Joe Rankin, the scout who had warned the fallen commander of his danger, stole away from the trenches and succeeded in reaching the open road to the north. His mission was to convey the tidings of the battle and call out relief for the beleaguered troops. The wonderful ride of this daring scout has become a feature in the history of the war. The distance from the scene of the massacre to Rawlins, the nearest telegraph point, is one hundred and sixty miles. Rankin started at ten o'clock Monday night on a strange horse, his having been shot in the battle, and delivered the startling tidings at Rawlins Wednesday morning between two and three o'clock, he having accomplished the distance in twenty-eight hours. This man brought the first news of the ambush and of the death of Thornburgh and his command.

The first morning of the siege broke bright and clear. It was a glorious day and the romantic scenery of the *cañon* never spoke greater glory to Nature. But the picture which the rising sun, as it moved across the arch, exposed to view, was one which none but a hostile could gaze upon and not shudder.

As the dark mantle of night was lifted and the first day of the siege came on, the orb of light was greeted by the groans of the dying, the moans of the wounded and the wild cry of the disabled horses. The hours of the first night had seen the soldiers labouring hard to complete their defence as far as possible and secure to themselves all the protection which the desperation of a forlorn hope could call upon men to devise. The location of the pits and wagons and the position of the trenches and wagons have been given. There were seventeen pits in all, about seventy feet long, two and a half feet wide and two feet deep, with breast works ranging from two to four feet above the opening and at its sides.

In the centre of the pits were forty-three wounded men, including a few settlers. One hundred soldiers occupied the pits and over two hundred and fifty dead animals surrounded the corral. There were two look-outs to each pit, making thirty-four men constantly on guard, through oddly fashioned loop-holes, in some instances made through the body of a horse.

As day grew on, the alert foe, securely hidden be hind the sheltering shelves of the bluffs, renewed their fire, watching each exposed point and directing aim at man or beast whenever carelessness or necessity brought them in even momentary view.

Captain Payne, then in command, during the night had the wounded horses shot for breastworks, dismantling the wagons of boxes, bundles of the bedding, corn and flour sacks, which were piled up for fortifications, so that the troops were fairly protected when morning came. The picks and shovels were used vigorously during the day for digging entrenchments. All the time a galling fire was concentrated upon the command from all the surrounding bluffs which commanded the position. Not an Indian could be seen, but the incessant crack of their Sharps and Winchester rifles dealt fearful destruction among the horses and men.

The groans of the dying and the agonizing cries of the wounded told what terrible havoc was being made among the determined and desperate command. Every man was bound to sell his life as dearly as possible.

About midday a great danger was seen approaching at a frightfully rapid pace. The red devils, at the beginning of the day, had set fire to the dry grass and sage-brush to the windward of the position of the pits, and it now came sweeping down towards the trenches, the flames leaping high into the air and dense volumes of smoke rolling on to engulf the troops. It was a sight to make the stoutest heart quail, and the fiends were waiting ready to send in a volley as soon the soldiers should be driven from their shelter. It soon reached the flanks, and blankets, blouses and empty sacks were freely used to extinguish the flames. Some of the wagons were set on fire, and it required all the force possible to smother the blaze. No water could be obtained, and the smoke was suffocating, but the fire passed, and the men still held their position.

All this time a constant fire was poured upon the pits, Captain

Payne being wounded for the second time and First Sergeant Dolan, of Company F, killed instantly; McKinsley and McKee killed and many others wounded. But the greatest danger was past. The men had now nearly covered themselves, but the poor horses and mules were constantly falling under sharp fire.

And so passed the first day. That night a second courier was sent out with despatches up to the hour of his leaving. There was great danger in breaking from the shelter of the trenches even under cover of the darkness, but the men who volunteered for this service knew no fear and were skilled in the intrepid feats they essayed. During the second day the bodies of the dead men and animals began to become offensive, and every opportunity afforded by a brief relaxation in the firing of the Indians from the heights which might indicate a temporary cessation of watching, the breastworks which crested the trenches would be increased in dimensions by the added body of a dead soldier or horse. Over these bodies dirt was thrown, and by this means the corpses were poorly buried and at the same time additional protection afforded the survivors of the fight. Thus had been erected three breastworks formed by the dead bodies of horses, while one was formed of dead soldiers piled one above the other and covered with earth.

Many were the earnest councils held as to the possible means by craft or daring of escaping the terrible pen in which the soldiers were. The hours were counted it would take the relief in which to reach the trenches, in case the couriers got through safely. There seemed no way but to wait the coming of the troops.

Just about sundown this day a charge was attempted, but repulsed, the Indians trying to drive off some of the horses that had broken loose. The attack ceased at dark, and pretty soon every man was at work enlarging the trenches, hauling out the dead horses, caring for the wounded and burying the dead. And so came on the third night. In the history of the siege this was the most uneventful night. Several trips were made for water, which brought no warning shot from the bluffs. The wounded were cared for and the protections made more secure.

The sun came up on the third day of the siege, shooting its rays upon the horde of dead, wounded and alive alike. How succour was prayed for; how the speed of the couriers was urged by the despairing soldiers as they contemplated their desperate, almost hopeless condition, rendered ten-fold wretched by the presence of their dead comrades and the sufferings of their wounded companions. But while yet the beleaguered troops were praying for the safety of their messengers and the hurrying forward of their relief, an outlook shouted alarm, and preparations were made for an attack from the foe which had been expected for hours. Every man jumped to his post ready to give the red devils a warm welcome. Even the wounded who were able to do so, grasped rifles and made ready to defend themselves, shattered as they were. But it was a relief, entirely unlocked for, but welcome beyond expression. It was the famous coloured cavalry under command of Captain Dodge, who had been intercepted by a Rawlins courier and had ridden to the support of their white brethren in arms.

The Dodge command had arrived at the entrance to the pass wherein the troops were entrenched before a note of their proximity had been conveyed to the Indians or the men in the pits. Here a halt was made, and Gordon, the mail carrier, and Sandy Mellen, from Middle Park, the guide, were sent forward toward the rifle pits to announce the arrival. The three men were challenged as they came in, and answered, "A company of cavalry." "That's a damned lie; it's an Indian ruse—look out," was the response from the pits. One of the advance then shouted, "I'm John Gordon," and the voice being recognised, they were directed to "come on in."

When the men in the pits heard that Dodge's company was near and that their couriers had probably reached Merritt, the poor fellows sent up a great shout, which was a sufficient signal for the coloured boys to come on, and the command made a dash for the pits. The shouting of the Payne men had aroused the Indians, and one or two shots from the heights were followed by a heavy and continuous volley in the direction of the pits. The dash was over a distance of 600 yards, and not a man was struck. Reaching the corral, the horses of the negro cavalry were quickly tied and unsaddled, and the men sank into the pits with their besieged comrades.

A soldier with Payne thus speaks of the arrival of Dodge and his coloured company:

> We were getting pretty d———d tired about that time. It was the third morning after we were corralled, and of course we didn't know whether any of our messengers sent out from camp had struck help or not. Suddenly that morning in the dusk we heard a noise. Even by that time some of us had begun to fear that the Indians would charge us, and we all then supposed it might be Indians. If it hadn't been for the voice of John Gordon, the

scout, who was riding in the advance, we might have poured in a volley at them; but you bet your life there wasn't no volley except cheers when Gordon rode in with five or six darkies alongside of him. Pretty soon he told us what was up and what to expect, and when Captain Dodge came up at a canter, leading the rest of his men, we didn't take much account, except to wonder a little at the colour of their faces. We forgot all about the danger of exposing ourselves, and leaped up out of the pits to shake hands all around. Why, (continued this soldier with curious *naiveté*), we took those darkies in right along with us in the pits. We let 'em sleep with us, and they took their knives and cut off slips of bacon from the same sides as we did.

Captain Dodge threw up pits to the east of the others, the work being accomplished very quietly be fore moon-up on the night following their arrival. As soon as Captain Dodge arrived the spirits of the beleaguered troops revived, and they became rather gay, and said if Merritt was coming no thousand Indians could take their pits. At night regular details had to make a sortie for water from the river, about one hundred and fifty yards away. The Indians would fire at random, but only two men were struck during the entire six days, and these only scratched. The Indians were in seven pits on the heights surrounding the little valley in which the troops lay hidden, and during the six days' siege became very skilful marksmen, doing sharpshooting that would do credit to the Creedmore. A soldier would take his hat, and placing it on a sword or stick, hoist it above the pits, and in five seconds it would be riddled with bullets sent from all directions. The soldiers got very few chances at the Indians, as they were well hidden, and so high up that good range was impossible.

Most of the Indians seen at a distance wore citizens' clothes, hats and all, many wearing uniforms taken from the bodies of the dead soldiers. On the second day of Dodge's rest in the pits, and the fifth day of the siege, a charge was expected from the Indians, as the soldiers had fired few shots the previous day, and the Indians evidently thought their ammunition was exhausted. But night came and went and no charge was made. During the two days that the coloured relief were in the trenches the only events to chase the monotony away were calling the hour, and an occasional shot at an exposed Indian. Little effort was made at jest or story-telling, as the presence of the dead and wounded chased away any desire for sport, and the stench from the dead animals and men was insufferable. One man by the name of Hogan essayed to make light of the situation, but the laughter was feeble and forced.

In this way, unwashed, unkempt, ill fed, at a time when even night, illumined by stars, refused its customary shield of darkness, the men of Payne's (white) and Dodge's (coloured) commands awaited further succour. They were not only beleaguered by savages, who kept a cross-fire on them from two commanding bluffs, but were listeners to constant insults, uttered in English and seeming to come from some white man quartered with their savage foes. When a horse or a mule fell a taunting voice from the bluffs would come, saying:—

"Better go out and harness him again for your funeral."

Again:—"Lift up your hats and give us a mark."

Still again:—"Come out of your holes, you ——, and fight. square."

This last from the renegade ensconced with the Utes.

The situation was chiefly horrible from the constant wounds and death-struggles of the poor animals, which they could in no way protect from the Indian fire. Says one:

Every few minutes you heard the dying gurgle of a horse or a mule, and although we fastened them as securely as possible at night, their pangs were such that they would often break away after being hit, threatening the men's lives in the trenches. Once a wounded horse leaped in his agony right into the pit we had dug for the wounded, where Lieutenant Paddock and seven men were lying at the time. It was a miracle, almost, that he did not trample them to death. As it was, we all opened a terrific fire on the bluffs, so as to make the Utes stop firing, and under cover of this fusillade a lot of our boys jumped up and hauled the horse out of the trench.

We had to watch out continually to give dangerously wounded horses and mules their quietus. If they got cavorting after receiving an Indian bullet, and we could see that they were maimed or fatally injured, the soldiers would take aim and finish them. It was awfully hard once in a while. A friend of mine got three flesh wounds in trying to save his horse's life. Finally, the horse was shot through one of his forelegs. Instead of writhing around like the others, he came hobbling up to the edge of the pit where Joe and I were and looked down at Joe, as if to say, "Help me, for God's sake!" Joe turned to me and said,

"You'll have to finish him, Hank; I can't do it; by God, I can't!"
I watched my chance as the horse turned and put a ball in right
behind his left ear, and dropped him. That night we hauled him
outside with the rest.

There were several pet dogs in the camp, among them a beautiful
greyhound, belonging to Lieutenant Cherry. The lieutenant says:

I used to let him out of my pit occasionally to run down to
the water. One night he came back with one of his paws shot
off. It turned out that he had been fired on by one of our own
sentinels, who mistook him for a crawling Indian. There was
nothing to do but kill the poor old fellow to save him misery.

One morning a soldier of Payne's command, wounded in the arm
and so ill that he had had no appetite for two days, turned to a negro
soldier close by him, saying, "Here, pard, stop shooting at them bluffs,
and for the Lord's sake make me a little coffee." The coloured hero
thus addressed answered not a word, but set to work. There was no
coffee in the pit, but there was some in the next one which was tossed
over. But how to make a fire without wood, that was the question.
The coloured man calculated the chances, made a break for the sutler's
wagon, snatched a loose side of a provision box and came back with
a bullet hole in the board, which was meant for his own body. Then
he made a fire in a corner of the pit and prepared the coffee for his
patient.

The sutler's wagon was a fair target, and the sutler himself was hit
in the leg while making an incautious approach to it. It had a lim-
ited supply of provisions, the regulation hard tack and raw bacon, and
a little liquor, which was of great service to the wounded. Another
vehicle which "saw service," and will doubtless be preserved at Fort
Steele as a pet relic of siege-history, is the ambulance taken down by
Major Thornburgh. It stood out with the wagons near the centre of
the oval space occupied by the troops, and is ventilated by some thirty
bullet holes. Rankin, the scout, got under it one day for a nap and was
awakened by a ball which struck one of the spokes within two inches
of the top of his head.

The horses of Dodge's soldiers were left standing, but before two
mornings had dawned nearly every one of the animals was lying dead,
three deep. All but four of the Dodge command's horses were picked
off by the Indians and these four were badly wounded. It was better to
have them killed than for them to be taken by the Indians.

THE SCOUT JOE RANKIN

Had the heights been accessible, Captain Dodge would have charged them with his company, while the others, including the wounded, covered him from the rifle pits, but this being utterly impossible, the ascent being nearly perpendicular, all that could be done during the day was to keep a good lookout from the loop-holes and return the fire when any Indians showed their heads. This, however, was a very rare occurrence, as the Indians had rifle-pits and loop holes. A very fortunate thing for the soldiers was that the Indians left them unmolested at night with the exception of an occasional shot to make them scatter to their pits. They were able, at great risk, to haul off the dead animals every night; otherwise the stench would have been intolerable. A sally was made every night for water, a distance of two hundred yards from the entrenchment.

The sixth night of the siege Private Eizer, of Company F, was shot in the face while out with a party after water. The Indians were only a few yards away, and were driven off by a volley from the guard and trenches. This night no courier could be got off owing to the constant firing of the Indians into the pits, but the troops determined to hold out if it took a month for succour to reach them. But they were confident that General Merritt, whose name was upon the lips of every one, was on the road to rescue them.

On the morning of the 5th about five o'clock, just as the grey streaks of day were pencilling the Eastern sky, the bugles of Gen. Merritt's advance sounded the officers' call, which is the night signal of the Fifth Cavalry. The men in the pits heard the glad notes with rejoicing, and impetuously turned out of their safety quarters to welcome the advancing rescuers.

As soon as the Indians saw Merritt's little army coming they fell back, and it is supposed held a council as to what to do. In the meantime firing had ceased entirely, and the men in the pits swung their hats, and danced and pranced and—ate like gluttons. General Merritt headed his command as it advanced to the pits. When he saw the wreck and carnage, the dead and wounded, and viewed the signs of massacre on every hand, he turned aside and wept like a child. This evidence of feeling on the part of the commander brought out cheers on every side, and while not unmindful of their dead comrades, the hour was one of rejoicing over the raise of the siege.

Several witnesses describe the arrival of Merritt and his troops, and say that when the general met Captain Payne, the two threw their arms around each other, and that tears were shed. That is not unlikely.

Both men were exhausted, Payne by his wounds and anxiety, Merritt by his long march. As for the rest, there is no concealment about the tears. There was such a scene in that wretched corral for five or ten minutes as few men witness twice in a lifetime, or want to.

A company of fresh men was ordered forward to the scene of the battle, about eight hundred yards south of the pits. In making this trip a lively skirmish took place with a band of concealed Indians, during which a considerable number of shots were exchanged, but only two men were killed and five wounded. In the midst of the skirmish, and to the surprise of every one, Brady, the white courier from Ouray and his Ute chiefs, stepped out from the brush on the mountain side, waving a flag of truce. Merritt permitted the courier to advance, and held a brief parley with him, in which the message to Douglass that the troops would go to the agency was delivered. While the talk was in progress firing ceased. Finally Merritt told Brady to "go back where he came from. He would not talk with him." The truce party then withdrew, and no more was seen or heard of the hostiles by the soldiers around Thornburgh Pass.

Lieutenant Hughes was one of the first to see Thornburgh's body, as it lay where it fell on the field of battle. The lieutenant says there were five or six wounds in the body, and that the scalp from the crown back was removed the only scalp taken in the fight or in isolated murders. Thornburgh was stripped, and lying on his back, and on his breast was a photograph of the young Chief Wammaniche.

It was discovered in visiting the battlefield after the siege that during the stampede of the wagon train by the Indians the trunk of Lieutenant Cherry, who covered the retreat and brought off the wounded, was secured by the Indians and broken open. They took everything of the contents but a bible, and left Lieutenant Cherry's picture in the trunk with the scalp of the likeness carefully cut out.

The force at the pass after General Merritt's arrival numbered all told 800 men—thirteen companies. The troops remained in camp three days, when General Merritt went south to the agency while Captain Dodge and his company acted as escort for the body of Captain Thornburgh and the wounded to Rawlins, which point was reached on the eighteenth.

In writing the account of the siege, which closes with the preceding paragraph, the arrival of the Dodge relief party and of Merritt's rescuing army is included. The exploits performed by these two commands and their wonderful marches to the trenches in the pass, present two of the most extraordinary events in the military service.

The courier who brought the news of the Thornburgh fight came direct to Rawlins and by 3 o'clock on the morning of his arrival, October 1st, the intelligence had been flashed to Fort Omaha. General Williams in less than a quarter of an hour was at work giving orders, consulting General Crook, who was in Chicago, and ordering matters forward. General Merritt, at Fort D. A. Russell, Cheyenne, was telegraphed to and ordered to the command of the expedition. The message was carried by the operator who received it at the latter place, to the general at his headquarters on horseback at break-neck speed. General Merritt at once began preparing for the expedition. The same was true of the arrangements at Camp Douglass, Salt Lake, and no time was lost, but everything perfected at short notice at Forts McPherson and Sanders.

This activity was also displayed by the Pacific Railroad. Though called to do almost extraordinary things it worked in harmony with the military, and the troops were all *en route* to Rawlins in a few hours, from which point succour was to be sent out. A special train of four cars of troops from Camp Douglass left Ogden at 2 p. m. of that day for Rawlins. Three hundred men and six hundred horses left Cheyenne the same hour for Rawlins. One company left Fort Sanders and two companies of cavalry left Fort Steele. The latter had their horses, baggage, etc., with them. Troops were ordered forward from Forts Fetterman and Robinson to leave for the seat of war as soon as they might reach the railroad, by special train. General Merritt, to whom the command of the expedition was given, was considered one of the best Indian fighters in the country, and his troops have accomplished wonderful things.

At 11:45 the morning of the 1st, he telegraphed to General Williams that he would be ready and start at 4 o'clock on the morning of the 2nd with a force of nearly five hundred and fifty men and animals, and provisions in plenty.

Early on the morning of the 2nd, General Merritt, at the head of four companies of cavalry, three hundred men, left Rawlins for the rescue, closely followed by five companies of infantry, two hundred and fifty strong, in wagons. Merritt was accompanied by Scout Rankin. On the 6th, Colonel Gilbert, of Fort Snelling, Minnesota, who had been placed in charge of Merritt's supporting column, left Rawlins with six companies of the Seventh Infantry, three companies of the Third, and three of the Fifth Cavalry; in all four hundred and forty men. Merritt's march to the rescue will be memorable as one of the most eager, energetic and rapid on record. The distance from Rawlins to the rifle pits is one hundred and sixty miles, and Merritt made the distance in forty-eight hours, transporting five companies of infantry in wagons. "*Old Wesley,*" it was said, would "*come with a whirl,*" and he did.

The experience of the Dodge command, while a small body of men, was none the less thrilling and exciting, and the intrepidity of their ride to the relief, after learning of Payne's situation, has been honourably mentioned by General Sherman.

The company, forty-three strong, under command of Captain Dodge, Lieutenant Hughes being next in command, left Fort Garland August 4, under orders to proceed to Middle Park and remain there as discretion directed, to prevent any collision between the settlers and the Indians. Camp was struck ten miles below Hot Sulphur Springs on the 19th of August Here the command remained until the 27th of August, when the troops proceeded to Peck's crossing of the roads leading to Rawlins and the agency. A halt of two days was made at this point for advices from the agency, when the command started back, as the rations were out. On the return route a communication was received to proceed to the agency to assist in the arrest of Indians under authority of the Agent. The command secured rations at Steamboat Springs and then took up the line of march for the agency.

On the 19th of September, Mansfield the courier from the agency was met. He bore the second of the three messages sent by Agent Meeker. On the 20th, the command started in quick time for the agency. The morning of the following day a slip of white paper was found attached to a bush by the side of the trail, with the injunction in large characters to hurry on the troops, as the soldiers at the agency had been massacred. This word, it was afterwards learned, had been left by a man named Clark, a ranchman. The Dodge command pushed on to Bear River, about ten miles further on, and here it was discovered that ranches had been deserted, and fleeing ranchmen who were met declared that the soldiers would be slaughtered if they proceeded. These messages and indications of the uprising only hastened the movements of the company and on they pushed.

While waiting on Bear River for the wagons to close up, Mansfield, the courier, again appeared, this time in company with Gordon, the freighter, whom he had met, and who bore messages from Captain Payne. The word conveyed was that the troops were corralled, with forty wounded men, and sorely pushed. Gordon was the third courier sent out from the beleaguered command, and Captain Dodge knew from this that the other two had gone on their errand to Merritt. Gordon himself bore a message to General Merritt, but it fortunately fell into Dodge's hands, at the same time assuring all that the two other messengers had gone on safely. After the receipt of this advice Dodge proceeded eleven miles, it then being dark, and pitched camp. It was the belief that they were watched by Indians, and they planned to go into camp as if intending to remain all night, and then during the darkness to steal away in their march to Payne's rescue. Gordon and Mansfield and a mail carrier from Middle Park, who had acted as guide, were with the command and aided in directing the ruse, and the course of the troops.

An hour after the night was on them, camp was broke, and the company, at first as quietly as possible, but soon after with abandon, rode as hard as possible in the direction of the Thornburgh ambush. The company rode all night, the wagons being sent to Fortification from Peck's, and just before daybreak, about half-past four o'clock, the command reached within hailing distance of the besieged troops. The ride thus accomplished was one of the bravest on record, not so much from the daring or exposure, as from its rapidity and the fact that every moment an ambush was looked for. The distance from the spot where the news of the Thornburgh massacre was received to the rifle pits was eighty miles by the trail followed, and it was accomplished in twenty-three hours.

CHAPTER 5

On to the Agency

Dispatches sent out from Rawlins on the 11th of October, based upon information which had been brought through from the front, stated that, having reached Milk River and relieved Payne's command, and recovered the remains of Major Thornburgh, General Merritt found himself unable to proceed further south, thus increasing tenfold the suspense felt concerning the fate of the people at the agency. It was stated that the Indians still occupied their formidable position on the bluffs overlooking the road, or trail, to the agency, and it was known that they had built fortifications and were prepared to resist an advance while taking very little risk upon themselves. Having no artillery General Merritt found that it would be almost impossible to dislodge the enemy. They occupied a position covering and commanding the only road passing through the Milk River Cañon. To illustrate the advantage of position occupied by the Indians, it is stated by those who were in the siege that an Indian, from his position in the bluffs, lying behind his breastwork, entirely safe and yet commanding a full view of the fortifications, killed forty horses belonging to Payne's and Dodge's commands.

Information had already been received, through Indian runners employed by Chief Ouray at Uncompahgre agency, that the Agent and the *employés* of the agency had fallen victims to the relentless knives and bullets of the so-called noble red man. It was also ascertained from the same source that the women had been made captives by the savages, and while every assurance was given that Mrs. Meeker, her daughter Miss Josephine, Mrs. Price and her two children, were entirely unharmed, there was still much room to doubt these stories, and every reason to fear the worst, while the best was hoped for. The report of the massacre of the male members of the agency was gener-

47

ally credited, but nothing certain was known. The greatest suspense prevailed upon all hands; hence the disappointment felt when the news was spread broadcast over the land that General Merritt would be unable to proceed to the agency until Colonel Gilbert, then at Fortification Creek with four hundred soldiers, should arrive to reinforce him. Twelve days had already elapsed since the massacre, and no news, except the unsatisfactory reports gathered from Indian runners, had been received.

But while the world at large was discussing this sad situation of affairs, General Merritt was solving the problem. In fact, he had really marched on to White River, and had become fully informed of the condition matters were in, before the news of the resistance of the Indians had been telegraphed abroad. The Indians remained in their fortifications until the runner left carrying the news above referred to, but deserted them soon afterwards, on the 10th. It is a well-known fact that they employed spies, who watched the progress of troops from the north, and who were thoroughly informed as to the steps taken to reinforce Merritt and supply him with provisions and ammunition. Seeing and appreciating resistance would be in vain, the hostiles suddenly withdrew, leaving the field to General Merritt, who lost no time in taking advantage of the situation and of pushing on to the agency. He accordingly took up his line of march and reached White River Agency, or the site of the agency, on the 11th of October, the very day on which the news that he would not be able to proceed had been given out.

The story which his march revealed is a sad one. It is a genuine frontier tale, as startling and pathetic as any of the works of fiction to which American border life has given birth. Sadder, because true. The people of Colorado have tried in vain, when perusing the bloodcurdling narratives as they have appeared from day to day in the newspapers, to imagine that they were reading stories which had had their origin alone in the hot-house brain of some sensational Indian storyteller. But we all knew "Father" Meeker, as the good old Agent was called. He was universally known, and his family and the employés at the agency were widely known of. The facts were facts; disagreeable but stubborn, and self-assertive. Hard as it was, we were forced to see that Colorado, a new, but one of the most prosperous and progressive States of the Union, had sustained an Indian massacre within her borders. General Merritt had not proceeded far on his march before he discovered this unpalatable fact.

When Mr. Meeker went to the agency at White River, he set about to make it in every way respect able, and being a man determined to do what was right by the Indians and the government, he was naturally anxious to surround himself with people in whom he could place implicit confidence. He accordingly selected as *employés* at the agency men, most of them unmarried, whom he had known at Greeley, all of them sober, industrious and intelligent. The white people at the agency were:

Agent N. C. Meeker.
Mrs. N. C. Meeker.
Miss Josephine Meeker.
Frank Dresser.
Harry Dresser.
Ed. L. Mansfield.
William H. Post.
Mr. and Mrs. Price.
May Price, aged 3 years.
Johnnie Price, aged 18 months.
Fred. Shepard.
George Eaton.
Young Thomson.

Of the males of this party, only Mr. Mansfield, if we except Mrs. Price's little boy, survives, (as at time of first publication). He owes his life to the fact that he was sent out with messages just previous to the massacre.

Signs of the work of the savages met the command at every turn after they left the scene of the siege. They left behind them the dead bodies of comrades in arms to find the corpses of the unfortunate men who had attempted to serve the government in a different capacity. The road was literally strewn with the nude and decaying remains of white men, whom chance had thrown in the way of the savages. The carcasses of innumerable horses were found, and the remains of one soldier passed lying by the roadside. The poor soldier had been stripped of all his clothing. On his left forearm was worked in India ink a star and shield, and on the right forearm the initials "A. B." In Fifteen-mile Cañon the ruins of several small trains employed in forwarding agency goods, notably the train of which George Gordon, of Rawlins, had charge, were passed. His loads consisted mainly of various sorts of agricultural appliances, hoes, spades, picks, shovels, and several sorts of wire fence.

To the fence the Utes are reported to have objected strongly, be cause their ponies injured their feet and legs on coming into contact with it, and they warned Mr. Meeker that he would not be permitted to put up any more of it. At this point Gordon, the freighter, and two of his train *employés* were killed, names unknown, and the bodies rest in one grave, marked with a rough board. A few miles further south are to be seen the charred remnants of a thresher and separator, and piles of broken crockery ware, while about the same distance north the Utes destroyed a wagon loaded with coffee and sugar, and at two other points are to be seen the remnants of burned trains.

The soldiers had marched but a few miles when the advance guard came upon another body, the remains of a white man, when, as the story was told to a correspondent of the Denver *Tribune*, who was on the ground, a conversation, of which the following is a report, oc-curred:

"What have we here?" asked one soldier of a comrade.

"It looks like the body of a man; and it is."

"It's a white man, too."

"To be sure it is, and terribly mangled and mutilated. The red dev-ils have got in their work on some unfortunate fellow."

Investigation revealed the fact that the body was that of Isaac Gold-stein, an Israelite who was called "The Jew," and whose proper name was known to but very few. Fortunately there was one soldier in the command to whom the old man had confided the secrets of his heart, and among others his great secret, the history of his own life, which though containing material for a volume may be related here in a few words and without marring this narrative, indeed as properly a part of it. Old Isaac was between fifty and sixty years of age but, he looked to be seventy. He was ever sad and uncommunicative, seeming to bear about with him a burden which, while it weighed him down, he did not care to share with others. But becoming friendly with this soldier, a private in General Merritt's ranks, he gradually confided the story of his romantic career to him.

In his early manhood Isaac Goldstein had loved a fair daughter of Israel as he loved not his own life. They lived in an eastern city, and a few months promised to see them united as man and wife. This young lady had a brother who had gone to California among the first who were attracted to the gold coast. At first he prospered and was cheerful and hopeful in his letters. At last he lost his health and was low spirited and despondent. His sister, whose name was Rebecca, determined at once to go to her brother to comfort, and, if possible, cure him. She had an opportunity to, and did, join the unfortunate party in its overland trip which perished at Mountain Meadow at the hands of the Mormons and the Indians combined. Isaac waited a long, long time for tidings of his love. At last the sad news of the massacre came. He at once came west to investigate the matter, and has here remained since.

He was never convinced that his Rebecca had been killed, but believed her to have been made a captive by the Indians. He determined to seek her out, and for many, very many, long years he had been searching and searching in vain for her, going from tribe to tribe, and gaining the confidence of the Indians that he might the more successfully prosecute the search. That the Utes now of Colorado took part in the Mountain Meadow affair is established almost beyond dispute. And thus, according to the story related by the soldier over the remains of the long, grey bearded old man as they lay on the hard sand-stones of the bottom of Milk River Cañon, came "The Jew" to be engaged in trading with Douglass's Indians.

The few auditors who gathered around the surviving friend of the old Jew, listened with interest and attention to the narrative. It was received with a sigh by all and derision by none. A few moments more and the remains of "The Wandering Jew" were hidden away in a trench dug for the purpose, and covered with earth, and the following legend appears on the simple stone grave mark:

ISAAC GOLDSTEIN.

KILLED BY INDIANS

SEPT. 29, 1879.

About two hundred yards from the spot where the body of old man Goldstein was found, the body of his trading companion, Julius Moore, a young man from Bainbridge, Mass., was also discovered, stripped of all clothing, and decaying, on the mountain side. Both Goldstein and Moore had been shot through the breast, and in the breast of each there were two bullet holes. Moore's body was badly hacked and mutilated. It also was buried.

Passing on a short distance the command came upon a coal mine, the mouth of which opened upon the *cañon*. Looking into this they discovered another body, which from papers found upon the person, was judged to be the body of Harry Dresser. He bore a letter from Agent Meeker, which read as follows:

White River, September 29, 1 o'clock p. m.

Major Thornburgh:

I will come with Chief Douglass and another chief and meet you tomorrow. Everything is quiet here, and Douglass is flying the United States flag. We have been on guard three nights, and will be tonight not that we expect any trouble, but because there might be. Did you have any trouble coming through the *cañon?*

N. C. Meeker,
United States Indian Agent.

The bearer of this message had crawled a short distance into the mouth of the shaft, where he was found dead, with his shirt bundled up for a pillow and under his head, he having died in that condition after having been shot in the head.

The soldiers also discovered in the fortifications of the Indians, the body of an unknown white man sitting in a squatting posture, with his gun in his hands as if ready to shoot. He is believed to have been a renegade who after fighting with the Indians, had been shot by them out of pure deviltry on the eve of their departure for the south.

A few hours march carried the command to the site of the agency. Of course every member was on the tiptoe of expectation—all anxious to discover what was to be found, and still all fearful to do so, because the worst was feared. The view which greeted their anxious gaze was one not to be for gotten. White River gurgled quietly on and seemed to be the only living object left. There was not even a breeze blowing to stir the tops of the trees which line the hillsides surrounding the beautiful Powell Bottom in which the agency was located. Everything was dead. The quiet of the grave reigned. The soldiers felt instinctively before reaching the actual location of the agency buildings that they were in the region of the lifeless.

So they were. The story of the finding of the nude and mutilated bodies of Father Meeker and those who had cast their lot with him among savage men and women, has already been printed in almost every newspaper in the land, and the sickening, but necessary details dwelt upon until the reader has been almost surfeited with the narrative. We will not linger over a picture so sad and disagreeable—a picture of the utmost loneliness, desolation, and death—a picture which has no bright side, not one pleasant corner.

All the buildings except one, the house which had been built for Johnson, had been burned to the ground. The Indians had taken everything except the agency flour and decamped. The women and children were missing, and nothing whatever could be found to indicate what had become of them. It was evident that they had either been murdered and buried or else taken away as hostages.

The Indian Agent, N. C. Meeker, was found lying dead about two hundred yards from his headquarters, with one side of his head mashed. An iron chain, the size of which is commonly known as a log chain, was found encircled about his neck, and a piece of a flour barrel stave had been driven through his mouth. When found his body was in an entire state of nudity, and was lying on the back. A bullet hole through the head indicated plainly the cause of death. The dead body of Mr. W. H. Post, Father Meeker's assistant, was found between the buildings and the river, a bullet hole through the left ear and one under the ear. He, as well as Father Meeker, was stripped entirely naked.

Mr. Price, the agency blacksmith, was found dead with two bullet holes through his left breast. The Indians had taken all his clothing and he was found naked. Thomson's remains were found burned to a crisp. His gun was found by his side. E. W. Eskridge was found about two miles north of the agency. He was stripped to an entire state of nudity, and had his head mashed in as if he had been struck over the head with some heavy appliance. Eaton was found dead. He was stripped naked, and had a bundle of paper bags in his arms. His face was badly eaten by wolves. There was a bullet hole in his left breast. Frank Dresser (a brother to the one found in the coalmine, as was at first supposed), was found badly burned. He had, without doubt, been killed instantly, as a bullet had passed through his heart.

The bodies were all buried and proper inscriptions placed over their graves. They will be allowed to remain where they now are until next spring, when they will be removed to the town of Greeley, where their friends and relatives will be allowed to drop a sympathetic tear upon their coffins, and their bones be permitted to rest among those of their kindred, and not in a strange and savage land.

CHAPTER 6

The Agency Massacre

This is the bloody chapter of our little history—the story of the butchery of the agency people by the Indians, the one great crime of the record. We have already seen that the savages had become greatly dissatisfied with Agent Meeker and anxious for a change. Their savage nature had not accepted with good grace the gentle manners and other reforms which he made an effort to introduce. The agent had commenced early in the spring to prepare for a good crop of wheat and corn. He had planted potatoes and onions and beans; had fenced the ground, dug wells and built irrigating ditches. But the Indians made serious complaint at these innovations, and did not hesitate to express their displeasure, not more in word than in deed. They made frequent protests to Mr. Meeker, and at last sent a delegation of four, which was headed by Captain Jack, one of the White River chiefs, to Denver, to lay the complaints of the Indians before His Excellency Governor Pitkin.

While in this city these commissioners from the Indian nation made no threats, but many complaints, bewailing bitterly that the Agent should attempt to plough the ground and his daughter to teach the young Indians the English language and the ways of the white man. They gave the governor to understand that they thought their civilization much superior to that of the white man, and said that they much preferred that the agent would give them their food and leave them to live their own lives.

During the entire summer, complaints were, being made of the hostile demonstrations of the Utes along the line of their reservation, north, east and south, and constant fears were entertained of an outbreak and massacre, at almost any small mining settlement in North Park, or along the Grand, Eagle, Gunnison, Dolores or Animas, while apprehensions were also felt for the fate of the stock raisers along the Bear and Snake rivers and in Middle Park. Two miners who ventured across the Indian line on the Blue River were shot down like dogs and other parties were fired upon for crossing over, and this at a time when the Indians were coming and going, hunting and camping and stealing, as suited them, on the white man's side of the line.

During almost the entire month of July, the country was on fire. From the Wyoming line to the New Mexico boundary, the great Continental Divide was a blaze of fire. Thousands of acres were burned over, and millions of dollars worth of timber on the reservation and off of it were destroyed, and game of all kinds driven out and burned. This the savages were not loath to acknowledge they did to spite the whites.

In this connection we cannot do better than to quote again from the account of Colonel Steele's visit to the agency, written since the horrible scenes of September 29th. Colonel Steele says:

Early in July last I was called to Rawlins, Colorado, to look after the mail route from that point to White River Agency. I remained at Dixon, on Snake River, several days. While there, Indians belonging to the Ute chief, Colorow's outfit, frequently came to Dixon to trade buckskin and furs for Winchester rifles, ammunition and other supplies. I learned that they were camped on Snake River, Fortification Creek and Bear River, from fifty to one hundred miles from their reservation. The Indians seemed to be quiet, but settlers complained that the Indians were burning the grass and timber, and occasionally killing their cattle and doing much damage to the country.

I also heard much complaint from the mining district near Hahn's Peak and Middle Park; that the Indians were burning the timber, and had burned the houses of several settlers and killed one man. Smoke was at that time plainly visible from large fires on the head-waters of the Snake and Bear rivers. On completing my business on the mail route, I returned to Washington. The first week in September I was called, (by disturbances on this mail route) to visit it again.

Arriving at Rawlins, Mr. Bennett, the sub-contractor for the route told me that he had attempted to establish his line of mail carriers on the route; that he had gone as far south as Fortification Creek, where he was met by Utes belonging to

Colorow and Ute Jack's band; that three Indians stopped him and told him that he must go back; that he parleyed with them and finally went on as far as Bear River, where he was met by more Indians of the same tribe, and though he fully explained his business to them, he was so violently threatened that he returned to Rawling without establishing the mail route. Bennett has freighted Indian supplies to the Ute reservation for several years, and knows many of the Indians. He was accompanied by a man who has lived among the Utes for years, and with whom they have heretofore been friendly.

Both advised that it would be dangerous to attempt to go to the agency. On the night of September 4th, I arrived at Snake River, and on the 5th went to Bear River, meeting no Indians on the way, but finding the grass and timber destroyed by fire all the way along the route. I remained at Bear River several days endeavouring to find parties to carry the mail to the agency. Many of the settlers were alarmed by the hostile actions of the Utes. Others anticipated no trouble, but all complained of the burning of the grass and timber.

On the morning of September 10th, I started with two mail carriers for the agency. We rode over the route followed by Major Thornburgh's command, and at noon rested at the mouth of the *cañon* where the battle has since taken place. Here at a tent occupied by an Indian trader, and two miles from the reservation, we met a number of Utes, one of whom asked where I was going. I told him to the agency. After a short talk with other Indians, he told me we must go back. I made no reply, but leaving one of the carriers at the tent, I proceeded up the *cañon* in which the Indians laid the ambuscade for Major Thornburgh's command, toward the agency. The Indians followed us to the agency. I afterwards learned that they belonged to Ute Jack's party.

On the return trip to Bear River I met many Indians going to the agency for the issue of rations. Several of the bucks hailed me, but I hadn't time to stop. At the trader's in the *cañon* I found several Indians purchasing supplies. At the crossing of Howard's Fork, thirty miles from the agency, I met three Indians, two of whom I saw at the agency the night before. They stopped me and inquired for ammunition for Winchester rifles. I replied, 'No sabe.' After detaining me for nearly one-half hour I persuaded them to let me pass, and reached Rawlins without further incident worthy of mention.

Having written this account of his experiences, Colonel Steele adds an opinion or two of his own, which are all the more forcible for coming from a government *employé*:

Eastern papers, the Secretary of the Interior and others are seeking some provocation for this outbreak. It was not the encroachment of miners, for there are none nearer than Hahn's Peak, one hundred miles away. It was not settlers, for there are none nearer than Bear River, fifty miles from the agency; they are few and scattered, and their only safety for life and property has been in retaining the friendship of the Utes. On the other hand, these Utes have since early summer been off their reservation from fifty to two hundred miles. They have destroyed all the timber and grass they could, have destroyed the property of miners near Hahn's Peak, and burned the houses and hay of settlers on Bear River; they have killed cattle belonging to settlers on Bear and Snake Rivers, and terrorised that whole region. They complained only that Father Meeker urged on them the benefits of civilization. I knew that these Indians meant war. Early in the summer they occupied the territory over which troops must pass to reach them. Slowly they retreated toward the agency, burning the grass to render it difficult for cavalry to operate against them. They purchased arms and ammunition of the most improved pattern and in large quantities. Within six weeks of the outbreak one trader sold them three cases of Winchesters and a large amount of ammunition, and the last Utes I met inquired of me for more. They gathered disaffected bucks from the Uncompahgre and Uinta agencies, and got mad because the agent at White River would not feed them. When everything was ready they assaulted Agent Meeker and shot at his *employés* to provoke an attack by the troops, and when the troops approached, with peaceful intent, to adjust the difficulty and right the wrongs of all parties, they laid an ambuscade and prepared to annihilate the whole command.

The trade in guns and ammunition with the Indians was unusually active during the entire summer. The post office for the Snake River settlement is at Dixon, about seventy miles south of Rawlins, and here there is a general Indian trader named Perkins, who is reported to have done more trading with the Utes this season than in five years before, and it is natural to suppose from recent accounts, that the bulk of it has been in war material. It is also said that the trader on Bear River (Peck) and Taylor, on Milk Creek, have had similar experience in this business with the Utes. Just the day before the Thornburgh fight it is reported that a party of Utes, headed by Jack, visited one of these traders and possessed them selves forcibly of a case of Winchester cartridges, saying they expected to fight the white soldiers on Monday.

All of this goes to prove that the White River Utes were expecting and preparing during the entire summer to fight, and had perhaps, long before the massacre occurred, determined to kill the agent. That they were no longer in doubt as to the course they meant to pursue after they ascertained that the soldiers were coming in, we are forced to believe. The assertion of Jack quoted above is proof sufficient of this.

The note found on the body of young Dresser, whose body was found in the coal shaft as above described, is another indication of this fact, though we *are* told that Douglass was flying the American colours. Mr. Lowry, the Snake River settler, who was among the killed in the Thornburgh disaster, on Sunday previous to the fight made his way to the agency, found the Indians in their war paint, dancing and about ready to massacre Meeker and family and the other whites there. He succeeded in arguing them out of their intention, however, by assuring them that there would be no trouble, and, having effected this, started back with difficulty to Thornburgh's command, reporting to the Major that if he pursued his march towards the agency the Utes would doubtless carry out their original intentions and massacre the agency people. The major, however, said he must obey orders, and his command was headed toward the agency when the bloody events transpired of which the reader has already had an account.

On that same day Miss Josephine Meeker wrote a letter to her sister at Greeley saying that all was quiet and peaceable again. Johnson had apologised to her father for his conduct, and expressed himself sorry for what had happened. She felt quite as safe there as in Greeley. The Indians had removed their women and children, and instead of there being one hundred and fifty *tepees* in the vicinity now there were only four. The military were expected every day, and Mr. Meeker had sent two Indians and a white man to meet them, but the Indians soon returned much alarmed. Mr. Dresser of Greeley also received a letter of the same date from his son Frank, who expressed himself similarly

N. C. MEEKER.

as to the safety of all at the agency. He said the only fear they had was that some of the Indians might set fire to some of the hay belonging to the agency, and to guard against this some of the boys mounted guard at night, otherwise they slept as soundly as in Greeley.

Before these letters had passed out of the Indian reservation, the massacre of the agent and *employés* and the burning of the buildings had been consummated. The Indians had been preparing, but secretly, for the worst. The removal of the squaws, which Miss Meeker seems to have regarded rather favourably than otherwise, was a very bad omen. The fate of the agency people was sealed then. The savages had already doubtless determined in council of war what plan to pursue, and could have foretold to an hour the fate of the few whites among them.

The dreadful day gradually approached. Thornburgh was expected to reach the agency on Tuesday at noon with the troops. The Indians, who at first were angry, brightened up, evidently at the thought of getting Thornburgh to Milk River Cañon. Douglass sent two Indians, with one white man, Mr. Eskridge, to meet Thornburgh.

On the morning of the massacre Douglass came to the agency and spoke of soldiers coming. Mr. Meeker said:

"Let them come. They will not hurt anyone. But we will send for all the chiefs and head captains and hear their complaints and talk the matter over."

Douglass did not say much and went away. The Indian Paveetz, husband of the notorious Jane, asked Mrs. Meeker on Saturday, Sunday and Monday if she was afraid. She said, "No," and each time he received the reply with a "knowing" look which it has since been very easy to translate into a warning or hint of the fate of the agency people.

Secretly the Utes were preparing for the massacre. Just before Eskridge left with the Indians, a runner was seen rushing up to the tent of Douglass with, as was afterwards learned, news of the soldiers fighting. Half an hour later twenty armed Indians came to the agency from the camp of Douglass and began firing. They seem to have marched quietly down from their camp to the agency quarters and without any extra "ado" began to deliberately shoot down the *employés* wherever found. Mr. Eskridge, who had been sent out with a second message to Thornburgh, was killed two miles from the agency, and the others were killed about the buildings, with the exception of Frank Dresser.

The firing began about half-past one, immediately after dinner at the agency. Douglass, the chief to whom so many good qualities were attributed before the outbreak and who has since proven himself to be one of the most cruel and heartless, as well as one of the most hypocritical of the savages, had eaten dinner with the *employés*. After the meal had been concluded he staid about the table, joking in a lively manner with Mrs. Meeker, Miss Josephine and Mrs. Price. He drank a little coffee and ate some bread and butter. Suddenly he turned around and went out doors. Mr. Price and Mr. Thompson and Frank Dresser were working on the building a few steps from the house and the chief joined them. He seemed to be in very good spirits and was joking with the men.

A few minutes afterwards the firing began. Mrs. Meeker and her daughter were washing dishes in one of the houses and Mrs. Price was washing some clothing at the door when the first report was heard. This was quickly followed by another. There came a volley of firearms a succession of sharp explosions. It was startling and all knew what was coming. Miss Josephine and her mother looked into each other's faces. Mrs. Price, who was washing clothes at the door, rushed in, exclaiming:

"My God! the Indians are killing everybody; what shall we do?"

Josephine said, "Keep all together," and the girl was as cool as if she were receiving callers in a parlour.

Just then Frank Dresser, an *employé*, staggered in, shot through the leg. Miss Josie said:

"Here, Frank, is Mr. Price's gun."

It lay on the bed. He took it, and just as they were fleeing out by the door the windows were smashed in and half a dozen shots were fired into the room. Frank fired and killed Chief Johnson's brother and wounded another Indian who was passing him.

Then began the great suspense. The windows were shot in and the bullets were flying everywhere. The first move of the poor women was to get under the bed in Josephine's room, to avoid the bullets, which were whizzing over their heads. Josephine had the key of the milk house and proposed to go there. The bullets were flying like hailstones, but the women and children and Dresser succeeded in reaching the place suggested, and they locked themselves into the house, which had double walls filled in with *adobe* clay, and there was only one little window. They stayed there all the afternoon, and heard no sounds but the crash of the guns. They knew all the men were being killed, and expected that the Indians would finish the day with the butchery of the women. Firing went on for several hours at intervals. There was no shouting, no noise, but frequent firing. While waiting in this horrid suspense Dresser said he had gone to the *employés* rooms, where all guns were stored, but found them stolen. In the intervals of shooting Dresser would exclaim:

"There goes one of the government guns."

Their sound was quite different from that of the Indians.

The party stayed in the milk room until it began to fill with smoke. While in the building they barely whispered, and tried to keep Mrs. Price's babies still. As the fire was increasing they left the milk house cautiously, and Josephine reconnoitred the enemy.

"It's a good time to escape," said she. "The Indians are busy stealing agency goods."

The shouting had ceased when, at about five o'clock they began to see the smoke curling through the cracks. Mrs. Price said:

"Josie, we have got to get out of here; you take May, I'll take baby, and we will try to escape in the sage brush across the road."

Miss Josie took May's hand and they went out, but first went into Mr. Meeker's room. It was not disturbed. The doors were open and the books were lying on the stand as he had left them. *Pepy's Diary* lay open on the table. It was at first thought by the party that it would be well to secrete themselves in Mr. Meeker's room, but they ultimately decided to try to escape then, as the Indians were busily engaged in stealing annuity goods, and as there was also a strong probability of their burning the house. They had broken open the warehouse and were packing blankets on their ponies. They started for the garden, when Frank said:

"Perhaps we can hide in the sage brush and escape."

He ran through the gate in the field with Mr. Price's rifle. He was near the field when last seen. Mrs. Meeker and Mrs. Price went inside the field through the wire fence. The Utes were so busy stealing annuity goods that they did not see the escaping party at first. About thirty of them, loaded with blankets, were carrying them toward Douglass's camp, near the river. The fugitives had gone one hundred yards when the Utes saw them. They threw down the blankets and went running toward them, firing as they went. Bullets were as thick as grasshoppers around the fugitive women and poor little babies. They tried to shoot Frank Dresser, who had almost reached the sage brush, but merely shot to frighten the women. However, Mrs. Meeker was hit by a bullet, which went through her underclothing and made a flesh wound three inches long.

As the Indians came nearer they shouted:

"We no shoot! Come to us! No shoot; white woman good squaw; come!"

Mrs. Meeker had fallen to the ground an easy prey. She was taken to Douglass's *tepee*, while Mrs. Price was taken possession of by an Uncompahgre Ute. The women and children were dragged across the irrigating canal and were wet to the skin when they reached the Indian camp. They were quite rough in handling their captives, but they said they would not hurt them.

As for the butchery of the *employés*, no white person survived who witnessed it. The women and children did not leave their hiding place until late, and when they did come out the cruel work had been accomplished. All was over. Mrs. Meeker in passing across the grounds passed the prostrate form of her husband, stripped with the exception of his shirt. She stooped to kiss for the last time the cold, blue lips, which had spoken so many kind and loving words to her in their married life of thirty-five years, but she was ordered by the brave Douglass to pass on. This one last simple tribute was denied her. The Indians say that most of the men took refuge in a house, and that they fired it and ran the white men out, killing them as they came. Their bodies were doubtless left where they fell, and we tell in the preceding chapter of how they were discovered by the soldiers.

There is one error which may as well be explained here. It was stated that Harry Dresser's body was found in a coal bank about twelve miles from the agency; this proves to have been a mistake. Josephine Meeker says that Harry was to have taken a dispatch from her father to Thornburgh; he was prevented from going, and when the shooting began was among the first victims. His brother Frank, after being wounded in the leg, managed to reach the house, and Josie gave him Price's gun. They all took refuge in the milk house and remained there several hours—until the smoke drove them to seek shelter elsewhere. In the milk house Frank said Harry and Eaton were the first shot. Frank and the women ran for the sage brush, he being a little ahead. The Indians, as soon as they saw them, threw down the agency goods they were stealing from the warehouses, and started for the fugitives, shooting as they ran, but they told the women to stop, they would not shoot them. Frank reached the sage brush. At this time he had on neither coat nor vest, and no shoes, consequently could not travel over the cactus. He had said that he should try to reach the troops that night, and must have gone back to the agency after dark and taken off the coat, vest and shoes from his brother's body, and then tried to reach the soldiers; he got as far as the coal bank, where he most likely encountered Indians and was again wounded by them and crawled into the shaft to die.

The bodies of the eight unfortunate men repose in a beautiful spot in Powell Bottom, underneath a clump of cottonwood trees and near the crystal waters of White River. The pines on the distant hillsides sing the requiem to the dead, when stirred by the soft winds of the valley. All is again peaceful and calm on White River. There are no Indians there, and nothing but dull, dead stones rise to assert the presence of the bones of the martyred men. They were honest, conscientious men, who died in the interest of mankind. They will live in the memory of their fellow-mortals.

CHAPTER 7

The Soldiers in Camp at White River

Merritt and his little army, now swelled by the arrival of Colonel Gilbert's detachment, started for the south on the 11th and went into camp three miles above the agency, headquarters being established and a supply depot located directly at the agency. The strongest company in the gallant regiment hardly numbered forty-five men, the smallest numbering twenty-seven men. As soon as the camp was located and the troops had commenced to recover from their hard march and exposure, scouting parties were sent out for a radius of fifty miles to ascertain, if possible, the camp of the Indians, but in no case were any "signs" discovered. As Merritt's orders had been simply to go to the agency, the commander made no further advance than an occasional reconnoissance in the direction the Indians were supposed to have retreated. In the meantime, while waiting for dispatches as to what course to pursue, reinforcements were gathering at Rawlins to be hastened on to Merritt's support.

Nine companies, under command of Colonel Brackett, had reached Rawlins, waiting orders to go forward. It was generally supposed that the hostiles had divided into small bands and scattered to different agencies, while the fate of the white women was, of course, still in doubt. No orders, except to restrain the Indians from violence and keep them at the agency, having arrived, General Merritt, on the morning of the 15th, at the head of seven hundred men, with ten days' supplies and in light marching order, started south, leaving Colonel Clifford with two hundred and forty men to guard the agency. The objective point was the camp of the hostiles who held the agency women, which by this time, it was concluded, was located on Grand or Blue Rivers.

The troops had only been on the march six hours when dispatches arrived at the agency for the commander. A courier at once started in pursuit of the army moving south, as the dispatches were of importance. They were orders suspending operations against the Indians and directing the withdrawal of the troops under Merritt to their proper stations in the Department of the Platte, leaving sufficient number of men at the agency to guard government property. General Merritt was to remain in command and await further orders, either at White or Bear River, as negotiations for peace were in progress, and it was understood that the hostiles would agree to surrender the captives and be made to deliver those warriors who had led the outbreak.

There was general regret felt all over the country and especially in military circles, that the outbreak was likely to be concluded without the troops chastising the red devils, and a universal feeling of disgust at the disgraceful termination of the campaign. If the Utes escaped deserved punishment this time it was felt that frontier settlers had no guaranty what ever that the Indians would not re-enact the same terrible atrocities at will.

And so the soldiers went unwillingly into quarters, returning to camp on White River on the 17th. The weather was very pleasant. The troops had a nice camp and very little sickness among the men. There were immense herds of cattle on the surrounding hills and the command was in daily supply of fresh beef. The flour found on the storehouse floor at the agency was issued to the troops.

It was believed everywhere at this time that no further demonstration would be made in the north and eyes were turned to the military in the south and the peace commission. But on the 21st two more gallant white men were sacrificed on the peace policy altar. The circumstances of the death of these two men were as follows:

It must be recollected that General Merritt had previously started, with nearly all of his force, from the White River Agency across the White River, intending to penetrate as far as possible southward with his wagon train. It was generally understood that no wagons could make their way south of the White River, but Merritt was too persistent a soldier to be dismayed by the maps and reports of those who had preceded him. He made for the White River Mountains, below the stream, and failed to find a pass for his wagon train. Almost at the moment when his wagon master reported to him the impossibility of making headway through the mountains, Merritt was handed by a courier, who had ridden from Rawlins, the dispatch peremptorily ordering him to halt.

Merritt, however, had his own reasons for ascertaining the state of affairs all around and below his command, in case he should be ordered to move on or in case he should be molested. Therefore he dispatched two companies of cavalry, under Captain Henry W. Wessells, Jr., and First Lieutenant William P. Hall, on the morning of the 20th inst., to effect a reconnoissance in force. A number of scouts, headed by Paul Humme, their chief, accompanied the command, whose double object was to learn whether the hostile Utes had made a permanent departure from the neighbourhood and whether there was any perceptible wagon road between the White River and the Grand River.

It appears that when the troops got some twenty-two miles below the White River Agency, Lieutenant Hall's command was attacked guerilla fashion by a body of Utes, who annoyed it till nightfall without stampeding it or doing it any injury, although the couriers report that two men were wounded.

First Lieutenant William B. Weir, Chief of Ordnance of the Department of the Platte, who was a volunteer on the expedition, attached to General Merritt's staff, had in the meantime left the command, along with the chief scout, Paul Humme, to hunt deer. Firing was soon after heard by the members of the main party, but nothing was thought of it until the long absence of the two men suggested the advisability of looking for them. After a brief search Lieutenant Weir's naked body was found where it had fallen, pierced by two bullets from rifles in Indian hands. Later on it was learned that he had encountered a war party of twenty savages by whom he had been killed and robbed, and at the same time Chief of Scouts Humme was killed. The cavalry found Humme's body on the 23rd and buried it. Both Weir and Humme were shot through the head, Weir being shot in the forehead and Humme in the eye. Weir's head was mutilated and Humme was stripped.

The Indian version of the fight is that a party of ten Indians had been stationed in the mountains to watch the movements of the troops on White River, and that on the 20th, about noon, a party of white men approached them; that watching the party from their places of concealment they allowed it to pass, believing it to be merely a hunting party from the soldiers' camp; that two of the party of white men fell behind and pursued some deer at which one of them shot, and that thereupon one of the Indians stepped out to see if the shot had taken effect, where upon one of the white men, probably Humme, shot and killed him; that several of the Indians having been discovered by the man who had shot one of them, he continued to fire upon them, whereupon as a last resort they raised the war-whoop, when the rest of the party of Indians rushed down from the mountains and attacked the party of six white men in a ravine, where one Indian was killed; that the party in the vicinity of the two men pursuing the deer killed both of them, and then went to the assistance of the others.

On the 23rd a battalion of five companies of the Fifth Cavalry, under Major Sumner, went into the mountains to the divide between the Grand and White Rivers, about eighteen miles south from where the fight occurred on the 20th, to reconnoitre, and here, with the troops excited over the butchery of Weir and his scout, and expecting another covert attack from the Indians at any moment, we leave Merritt and his command and pass to the consideration of other events, crowding fast upon each other.

CHAPTER 8

The South

Thus far in this history little has been said regarding the movements of the troops in the south or the condition of affairs at the southern agencies. News of the uprising at White River reached Los Pinos by runner the same day that Scout Rankin got into Rawlins. The day that the outbreak occurred, Chief Ouray had started on a big hunt, which was to have lasted three months, but the news carried through to him by the runner in twenty-four hours caused his speedy return to the agency.

Ouray had always been a firm friend to the whites, and this horrible massacre caused him great grief. People everywhere felt assured that if any effort of his could save the imperilled lives of those at the seat of war they would be saved, and his past reputation led all to believe that should there be danger of an insurrection among the Uncompahgre Utes, the people would be warned by him. He called in all the hunting parties which were out, intending to keep them under his own eye, and not let them have any connection at all with their brethren of White River.

Immediately upon the intelligence reaching the Los Pinos Agency, Major W. M. Stanley, agent, sent Joseph Brady to the White River Agency, accompanied by a bodyguard of fifteen Utes sent by Ouray. Ouray sent a positive command to the hostile Utes to cease fighting, the order reading as follows:

To Chiefs, Captains, Headmen and Utes at White River:
You are hereby requested and commanded to cease hostility against the whites, injuring no innocent persons or any others further than to protect your own lives and property from unlawful and unauthorised combinations of horse thieves and

desperadoes, as anything further will ultimately end in disaster to all parties.

(Signed)

Ouray,
Head of Ute Nation.

Brady, who is a young man and unaccustomed to any continuous exertion, stood the terrible ride nobly, not one halt being made between the two agencies. It required a great deal of courage to start out immediately upon hearing the horrible news from White River, and go there with no other protection than a band of red men directly allied to the assassins, with the noble hope of trying to save the lives of the remaining whites; and this is exactly what this young man did. On his return from his mission he spoke in the highest terms of Sapavanaro's kindness to him on the journey, and said that nothing would induce him to believe anything but that this chief was a warm friend of the whites. "Give the devil his due."

Following the dispatching of this order came start ling rumours from the south to the effect that Ignacio, at the head of one hundred bucks, had left for the north, and that Chief Ouray was powerless to control his young men. It was reported that three hundred Southern Utes were on the war-path, and the inhabitants of the frontier settlements became greatly alarmed for the safety of themselves and homes. The militia of the south was organised, arms were sent to them and General D. J. Cook, of Denver, was placed in charge of the State troops below the divide. At the same time application was made to General Pope for regular troops to be sent to the southern agencies.

Likewise in the west came daily rumours of the proximity of Indians. At Fairplay, Alma, Breckinridge, Eagle River, Twin Lakes and other points, citizens and settlers prepared for an attack from the hostiles, it being generally feared that the White River tribe, after being repulsed by Merritt's advance, would scatter and fall down in small bands upon the exposed and more isolated settlements and camps along the main range. General Joe C. Wilson was placed in charge of the State troops in the South Park and Gunnison countries, and reported within two days that he could send out nearly any number of men required for the defence of the people and towns along the carbonate belt. A large amount of arms and ammunition were forwarded to Leadville, where General Wilson established his headquarters. Chapters could be written on the different "scares" which sprang up from this direction.

The most extravagant reports of danger came also from Middle

Park and that section, and campers, herders, and prospectors "came in" in a hurry. General W. H. Hamill was ordered to the command of the militia in this section, and with arms forwarded from Denver went from Georgetown to Middle Park and armed all the people on the frontier and within the line of possible attack. State companies at George town, Central and other points, were placed under arms and a system of scouts and runners established, which would assure the earliest news of any danger at remoter points.

It may be as well to state here as anywhere in this work that only one or two stray Indians were even seen, and that no loss of life or property transpired in the Eagle River, South Park or Middle Park countries during or succeeding the White River uprising.

But while the condition of affairs at the northern agency and the fate of the women captives were in doubt and uncertainty, public attention was attracted to proceedings in the south, where the utterances and opinions of Head Chief Ouray were eagerly watched for, and weighed as having the deepest significance. The well-known friendship for and loyalty to the government of this old chief gave to many the assurance that what he said might be relied upon, and what he prophesied might safely be anticipated. Numerous stories came from the southern agency, or credited in their source to that point, that Ouray could not control his people and had warned the settlers in the south to be on their guard; that many of Ouray's immediate followers had forsaken him, and that bands of New Mexico Indians were swarming into the Uncompahgre country to form conjunction with the red raiders of the north and declare general war.

As these reports came to the more thickly settled sections, and were taken up by the press of the State, the numbers of Indians engaged or in sympathy with the revolt increased gradually, until it was currently stated and generally believed that fully two thousand Indians were on the war-path, with accessions gathering from Utah tribes, the Northern Arapahoes, Bannocks, Shoshones and other nations. As a large part of the Ute nation was located in the vicinity of the San Juan country, and as two influential chiefs lived in that section, actual developments from the south were awaited with deep anxiety, especially as it was believed that the rapid hurrying of troops toward the Los Pinos and Uncompahgre agencies would have a tendency to precipitate any threatened uprising among the southern bands.

The first really authentic information as to the actual situation of affairs among the Indians of the south; the sentiment of the head men and the position of the principal chiefs, reached the capital of the State in the shape of a letter from the clerk for the agent at Los Pinos Agency, received October 9th, in which he said:

> Chief Ouray was at the agency this morning, accompanied by a special messenger from Chief Douglass, of the White River Utes. The messenger left on the evening of the 2nd inst., with instructions to Ouray to have no fears of any trouble from his tribe; that the fight now going on is an affair of their own, and do not wish anyone to interfere. They propose to settle it without any assistance from outside parties, and in any event will not trouble him or his people. That the three women and three children, one a babe, are safe at his house, shall be well cared for and released as soon as the fight is over.
>
> The money and papers belonging to the agency have been turned over to the Agent's wife. A messenger sent out by Ouray, who arrived at the same time, reports that the troops are strongly entrenched and still fighting; that with the supply of provisions on hand he has no fears of their ability to hold out until reinforcements arrive.
>
> I am requested by Chief Ouray to state to the people of Ouray and vicinity that they need have no fears whatever from the Indians of the Los Pinos Agency; that none of his people took any part in the affair at White River, and that they are desirous that the peaceful relations which now exist shall forever be maintained; that in case any danger threatens us he will immediately notify the agency and the people of Ouray; that he deplores the trouble existing at White River, and is extremely anxious that no further fighting or bloodshed shall take place, and will use his utmost endeavours to bring about a speedy settlement of the present difficulties. Any information he may receive will be immediately communicated to the agency and promptly forwarded to Ouray City.
>
> Ouray's word is 'legal tender' in this valley, and I trust it will have its effect and quiet, in a measure, the excitement which now exists.
>
> > Yours, respectfully,
> >
> > > George P. Sherman.

General Edward Hatch, commanding the department of New Mexico, was ordered to assume charge of the forces in Southern

Colorado, which promptly, on application to General Pope, of Fort Leavenworth, were rapidly concentrated at and below Alamosa. General Hatch remained in command of the Southern Colorado troops until the appointment of the Investigation Commission spoken of in the succeeding chapter, when he withdrew, and General McKenzie, of San Antonio, Texas, was appointed in charge. Troops were located before the outbreak at Forts Garland and Lewis, where permanent posts were established. These were at once ordered to prepare for march and to await commands from headquarters.

Troops were ordered from San Antonio and Fort Clark, Texas, Fort Hayes. Kansas, and Fort Union, New Mexico, to Southern Colorado and Northern New Mexico, to protect the settlements and advance the war in Colorado, and at the same time to frustrate the hostile demonstrations of the Indians in New Mexico. By these movements quite an army of regular troops were formed for march to the frontier in the south, their plan of operations being to protect settlements, check uprising and co-operate with Merritt in the north.

When this sub-department or column was placed in charge of General McKenzie after the recall of General Hatch, at which time its maximum strength was reached, the force numbered one thousand men and was officered as follows:

General McKenzie commanding; John F. Guilfoyle, Ninth Cavalry, Assistant Adjutant General; Second Lieutenant Charles W. Taylor, aid.
Battalion of four companies of the Twenty-second Infantry, Major A. L. Hough, commanding.
Company H, Fifteenth Infantry, Captain J. W. Bean.
Detachments of Companies I and B, Fifteenth Infantry, First Lieutenant George A. Cormick.
Battalion of mounted troops, Captain James H. Bradford.
Company G, Nineteenth Infantry, Captain James H. Bradford.
Company K, Ninth Cavalry, Captain Charles Parker.
Surgeons, Dr. J. H. Collins and Dr. x F. H. Atkins.

The positions assumed by the troops were arranged so as far as possible to cover as wide a scope of country, and, at the same time, have the column as compact as such a plan made practicable; the main body, or rather the largest body of troops, proceeding to a point in the vicinity of the Indian villages near Animas City, from which point by trail and road it is but eighty miles to Ouray. The troops from here could strike the Dolores trails readily, and were in a position to cover the settlements and strike quickly and hard, should the Indians make a break.

In this condition affairs in the south, like those in the north, remained passive for some time. Merritt at White River guarded that frontier; the State militia, armed and equipped, protected settlements; General McKenzie and his forces swarmed along the frontier in the south. It was well known at this time that the Indians engaged in the White River massacre were on Grand River, and in probable possession of the white women. The hostiles were hemmed in on three sides and had but two alternatives: to surrender or take flight along the valley of the Grand to Utah, and seek refuge in the wilderness in the southern part of that territory or the protection of their relatives, the Uintas.

CHAPTER 9

Josie Meeker Makes Her Escape

On the evening of October 14, General Charles Adams, Special Agent for the United States Post-office Department, received, at Denver, telegraphic notification that at the request of Secretary Schurz he had been detailed for special work as representative of the Interior Department among the Indians. A second dispatch from Washington gave General Adams specific instructions as to his mission and how to proceed. His principal, overshadowing duty was the rescue of the captive white women. The appointment was regarded with great favour. General Adams was agent for the White River Utes in 1870-1, and was the first Civil Agent of the Los Pinos tribe, acting in that capacity during the years 1872-3-4. His intimate knowledge of the Indian character, his bravery, energy and sagacity, it was felt, would be equal to any demands his errand might make upon them.

The general said very little as to his plans, and the people at large were ignorant of his intentions or movements until he commenced to act, when the history of his course became public. This much was understood, however: that he was to proceed directly to the hostile camp and demand the immediate surrender of the women, if in camp, and that the hostiles lay down their arms. If these demands were not acceded to, General Adams was to at once withdraw and notify the Department and the military. The tenor of Secretary Schurz's *pronunciamento* left no doubt as to the contingent proceeding on the part of the government; the Indians then had to be brought to justice and by the military. The troops would take care of the hostiles, while General Adams would endeavour to keep at peace those Indians who were not engaged in the Meeker-Thornburgh butchery.

In the event of the acquiescence of the Indians in General Adams' demands, it was not understood that they were to be accorded leniency. The General was to hold out no promises except the general one that their good conduct would be reported at Washington, and prompt compliance with the demands would be taken into consideration by the government.

General Adams left Denver October 15th for Los Pinos.

Two days after he was followed by W. J. Pollock, United States Indian Inspector, who was to officially investigate affairs at the southern agencies. Major Pollock was accompanied by Ralph Meeker, a son of Agent Meeker, who, armed with special authority from the Interior Department, hoped to assist in the recovery of his mother and sisters. Messrs. Pollock and Meeker expected to join General Adams, but were prevented from so doing and proceeded to Los Pinos, where they remained.

General Adams arrived at Chief Ouray's camp on the night of the 18th, where he had a long conference with the head of the Ute Nation, and with his aid and advice perfected his plans for the trip to the Grand River one hundred miles north, where the captives were then known to be. The following day General Adams arrived at Los Pinos and began active preparations for his perilous and important journey. Ouray accompanied the General to the agency and assisted him in arranging for his departure.

On the morning of the 19th General Adams started north for the Grand River country. His escort consisted of three chiefs and ten Indians. The chiefs were named Sapavanaro, Shavano, and Young Colorow. He was accompanied by Count von Doenhoff, Secretary of the German Legation at Washington, an intimate friend of Secretary Schurz, by a special correspondent of the *Denver Tribune*, and Captain Cline, an old scout and frontiersman. There were also two white men along to drive wagons and take care of the camping outfit.

A provision wagon and buck board were taken along, in order that the ladies might be spared the fatigue of a long return journey on horseback. With great thoughtfulness, Ouray had sent along his own tent for the use of the ladies.

The route taken was the wagon road, built by Johnson's army in 1859, to Utah, which was followed for forty miles beyond the Gunnison River, where the wagons were left, and the remainder of the journey performed on horseback.

The party secured an early start and travelled forty miles, to the crossing of the Gunnison River, on an old Mormon trail, the first day. Here two runners were sent ahead by Sapavanaro to inform Chief

Douglass of their approach, in order that he might collect his head men and consult with them before the arrival of the envoy. The next day they reached Whitewater Creek, thirty miles further, arriving there about two o'clock. A halt was made until sundown when the ride was resumed, and they got to Grand River that night. At noon that day two Indians met them. They were Cojoe and Henry Jim. They were from the hostile camp, and told the party where the camp was, and that the women were all safe. The Indians also told where the women were kept and in whose tents they were.

The next morning, the 21st, the general and his escort left Grand River and struck the hostile camp about ten o'clock. It was twenty miles distant from the river. Shortly before they reached there one of the two Indians sent ahead returned and said that, after a whole night's council, the Indians had concluded to let them come in. Douglass and some of his men, they said, would meet them. When they got to the camp General Adams discovered that the women were in a small camp on Plateau Creek. The main camp was at the mouth of Roon Creek, on the Grand River. Adams went to the small camp, composed of about fifteen lodges, and proceeded to the further end. There were three tents, and in each tent a prisoner.

"Ugh! Ute house; pretty soon see white squaws," said Sapavanaro.

So at last they had arrived at their goal in just six calendar days from the time General Adams left Denver.

The general, who was in advance, rode first toward the farthest group of *tepees*, and stopping at one, in the doorway of which stood a squaw, asked if the white squaws were in there.

"*Katch*," (no), was the reply, and General Adams started for the other tent, when, "Hold on, General," exclaimed Captain Cline, excitedly, "I see one of them."

"Good," said the General, "keep an eye on her," and rode off to the other tent. This was entirely empty, and he rode back to the first.

The lady whom Captain Cline had seen, in spite of the efforts of the squaw to conceal her by standing in the door, then came out, exclaiming:

"Oh, have you come for us? I am so glad."

She then said she was Miss Josephine Meeker; that this was the camp of Chief Johnson; that her mother, and Mrs. Price and little boy, were in the other *tepee*, Josie having the little girl with her. After a few moments conversation, General Adams told her that he would return in a short time, and rode off to the other tents. One of these was empty, and the other entirely closed, save a small opening in the doorway. Before this the party dismounted, and then began an excited colloquy between Sapavanaro and the occupants of the tent, he seeming to speak angrily and indignantly, and the other speakers, who afterward proved to be Captain Billy and Waro, both Uncompahgre Utes, answering in a sulky way.

Presently Sapavanaro turned to General Adams and told him in Spanish that, seeing them coming, the women had been hid, and that only the unlooked-for move of his in riding to the fartherest tent first had prevented them from hiding Miss Meeker.

They had sent for Douglass, whose camp was about sixteen miles distant, and nothing could be done until his arrival. Upon this information, saddles were uncinched and horses were picketed for a stop. While waiting the party had a fine opportunity to observe the camp and its surroundings.

The plain upon which the tents were pitched was as fine pasture land as Colorado contains, and extended in three directions as far as the eye could reach, mountains rising on the other side, and a small creek flowing within fifty yards of the tents. Upon a small stand set up between the tents hung a non-commissioned officer's sash and a cavalry sabre, topped by a uniform coat; several army saddles were piled in front of the tents; mules and horses with the United States brand on them were grazing on the *mesa*, while government blankets, bags of flour, etc., were scattered all around.

The escort, the Uncompahgre Utes, save only Sapavanaro and Shavano, who stood aloof, mingled freely with their white brethren, and were soon laughing and talking loudly.

After perhaps an hour's waiting, a short, ungraceful Ute rode up, followed by two others. Though commonly dressed, yet a brightness of face about him and the hushed talk of the Indians around prepared the party to be told that that was Douglass.

Dismounting from his horse he spoke to General Adams, shook hands with him and the rest of the party, and then turned away and became absorbed in a consultation with Shavano and his two head men.

This lasted a short time, when Douglass went up to General Adams, who, seated on the ground, had been quietly waiting for him to open the negotiations, and kneeling on the ground, drew a map of White River and the surrounding country with his finger. He then explained that the troops were continually advancing and his men retreating before them; that neither he nor his men wished to fight, and concluded by requesting the general to go to White River and tell the soldiers to stop their advance.

To this General Adams replied that he had been sent by the government to tell him that it wished for no war; but that the "white squaws must be returned to their friends."

"I give you white squaws, you go to White River?" asked Douglass.

"Yes."

"White squaws stay here till you come back?"

"No," replied General Adams, "white squaws start tomorrow *home*. I go today to White River."

Douglass thought a moment, then, rising, said to the general:

"You come in," and went into the *tepee*, which had during the conversation become filled with Utes. General Adams followed, and seating himself, there began a council which lasted for five hours.

General Adams furnishes the following account of the proceedings council *tepee*:

There were about fifty chiefs in the tent. I was supported, as you might say, by Chiefs Sapavanaro and Shavano, who were under my charge at the southern agency, and there was also present Sawawic, a chief whom in 1870 I nursed for three months in my own house at the southern agency. I formally made my errand known, and then one chief after another spoke, nearly all of them refusing their consent to the surrender. The pipe was passed around, but I refused to smoke with them, and so did Sapavanaro until they had consented to a release. Finally Shavano became angry and discouraged and arising from the council told me it was useless to parley further, and left the tent.

At this Sapavanaro stepped into the circle and made a most powerful and determined speech, more of a threat, than an appeal. During his great talk there was considerable excitement and *powwow* in the council, but I learned later that the chief said that he bore the mandate of Ouray. The Indians must surrender the captive women to General Adams or they would not be recognised by Ouray. They would be shut off from communication with their head chief; not allowed to come to his camp, and Ouray would join with the white soldiers and force the surrender or drive the rebellious Utes from the country.

This speech had a deep effect, and an old Uintah chief who was in the council held private conversation with Chief Douglass, evidently urging him to obey Ouray as the politic course. Douglass then arose, and after endeavouring to get me to go with the troops first and then return for the prisoners, but being again refused, he finally yielded an ungraceful assent. Then one after another of the opposing chiefs followed suit and the agreement became nearly unanimous.

I saw Cojoe, an Uncompahgre, in the council. He wore Lieutenant Cherry's dress coat and his watch and chain. I think this chief had three or four men in the camp. There were probably ten or twelve Uintahs in the camp. Of these latter there had undoubtedly been many more at first, but they fled to the west when the message from Ouray was received.

At the close of the council the long pipe was passed around, and General Adams came out, saying to his company that the ladies had been sent for and would be here in a few moments.

Presently there came toward the white men an old lady leaning on a stick, whom they knew at once to be Mrs. Meeker. Mrs. Price followed her, her little boy being carried behind in a blanket, Indian fashion. They shook hands cordially with Adams and the others.

"We are so thankful you have come," they said. "Yesterday a runner came in, and a little while after we were told that Washington would be here tomorrow; but the Indians had so frequently told us things of that kind to torment us that we hardly believed. But now we can't help believing it. When are you going to take us away?"

"Very soon," said General Adams. "I have arranged everything so you can start tomorrow."

"We are so glad," said Mrs. Price. "When the Indians came to our tent and made us go into that brush we didn't know what was going to happen to us; but we had become so hopeless that we didn't care much."

In a few moments General Adams rode off with Douglass, Sapavanaro, and Shavano. He was to go to the camp of Douglass that night, and in the morning start for White River. Count von Doenhoff accompanied him. Before he left, Douglass ordered Miss Meeker and the little girl to be brought over to where the rest were; and when they came there was a joyful reunion on the part of the ladies.

One of the *tepees* was prepared for their sleeping accommodation, and they early retired to rest to prepare for the necessarily early start next morning.

After the women had been given up, and in company with the twelve southern Utes who had accompanied the envoy to Grand River, had started south, General Adams took a guard of twenty-five White River Utes and, in company with Chiefs Sapavanaro, Shavano and Sawawic, started for Merritt's command, to stop their march south. When about twenty miles below the agency the party were discovered by Merritt's scouts, who reported, as was afterwards learned, that a band of Indians were approaching. Before Adams was aware of his proximity to the soldiers the party were surrounded, and, as he believes, escaped fire by a moment by their discovery of Adam's flag of truce, which he at once raised. The Indians were positive he had been treacherous, and showed every manifestation of anger and bitter resentment.

But the faithful Sawawic exhibited his confidence in the General, and reassured the others by dismounting and proceeding forward alone. Adams sent word to the soldiers and the bugle call was sounded. The Indians had clambered up the mountain side and were waiting developments, and the general turned back for them. Just as he had prevailed upon Shavano to come to his side, a squad of soldiers, who had not heard the bugle sound, rode up, when Shavano with a yell again bounded away, and it was some time before Adams could get his escort together again. The party proceeded to the agency, and General Adams told General Merritt what he had accomplished and promised. Merritt at once withdrew his advance, and Adams and escort returned to the Grand River camp, the escort reporting what Adams had done, which was satisfactory evidence that he had fulfilled his agreement.

General Adams proceeded next day towards Los Pinos, and arrived at that agency October 29th.

CHAPTER 10

Going Back

During this time we have left the women, Mrs. Meeker, Miss Josephine and Mrs. Price, and Mrs. Price's babies, in the hands of the hostiles. Twenty-three days have elapsed since they were made captives, and they have passed through an experience which seems in every way incredible. That they should have borne up under the trying ordeal of this time is the wonder of the day. The experience at the agency, the imprisonment, the massacre, the treatment they received at the hands of the savages, the dread and anxious state of mind which must have been continual with them from beginning to end, were sufficient, it would seem, to break down the strongest organisations. During all this time thousands, millions, of anxious eyes have been turned towards the western border of Colorado, peering into the wilderness and the mountains, to discover some trace of the captives.

An occasional glance which was only sufficiently plain to strengthen hope and create doubt was afforded, thus heightening rather than lessening the suspense of the nation and in creasing the sympathy and anxiety felt for the poor wanderers in a strange land among a wild and savage race. Once in a while there came statements from the Indian runners, who were constantly plying between the camp of Chief Ouray and that of the hostiles, saying that they were safe in the hands of the White River Utes at a spot some hundred miles north of the Uncompahgre, or Los Pinos, Agency. But the statements of the Indians were not considered strictly reliable, for, while it was thought they were held as captives, it was doubted whether they had been treated with any respect or indeed whether their lives would be spared.

The story as told by the rescued captives is a pathetic and an absorbingly interesting one. It is a strange and peculiar story—a new picture of Indian life and of the Indian land, full of light as well as of shadow, abounding in bright and sunny spots, we are pleased to say, as well as in dark and gloomy corners—in streaks of sunlight as well as in thunder storms. It is a revelation, a new account of the life and manners of the aboriginal American, the noble red man of the Rocky Mountains. The stories of the captives as told to General Adams, and as afterwards related a hundred times over by the captives to their friends and the press, give glimpses of Indian life more curious and instructive than anything which has appeared in the press or in literature for the last thirty years.

A great deal of picturesque Indian life is painted in Cooper's novels, but that is either fiction or facts so embellished and heightened as to be undistinguishable from the veriest romance. In the reports we have had of the incessant Indian wars in recent years, the barbarities of the native tribes have made a great figure, but there have been few relieving features, and little light has been shed on the kind of life which the Indians lead among themselves. These are narratives of thrilling interest which lift the curtain and disclose phases of savage humanity as it exists in the far-off western wilds, and enlarge our knowledge of Indian character as it exists at present. Public attention has been chiefly fixed on the massacre and the rescue, but since the women and children who were carried off are out of danger, a singular interest attaches to what happened to them while they were in the power of the savages and to the knowledge they gained while in that hapless condition.

The minute and interesting recitals of Miss Meeker, Mrs. Meeker and Mrs. Price, form the most valuable contribution, to our knowledge, of the interior life of the Indians which has been made in this generation. During their captivity of twenty-three days these ladies had opportunities to observe the character and the strange antics of their captors such as have not before occurred in our time, and, it is to be hoped, will never occur again to persons of their sex.

To begin with the beginning, we must retrace our footsteps, and ask the reader to return with us to White River. We will not stop to listen to the moaning of the winds, the lowing of the agency cattle as the sun descends on that sorrowful day, or to moralise over the ashes of the agency buildings or the dead bodies of good "Father" Meeker and his faithful followers. For the present we leave these things to those who have not the living to care for. We leave the dead to bury the dead, while we pursue the captives on their wild course into the mountains.

Having massacred the men at the agency and burned all the buildings but one, the savages set themselves to work to secure the plunder and carry it away. As we have already seen they had removed their women to a place south of the agency, that they might be out of danger in case the soldiers should push through and attack them. To the squaws' camp later in the day they repaired.

When the women rushed out of the burning building, driven from their hiding place like foxes from their dens by the sportsman, and made the one despairing dash across the open field, hoping to cover themselves in the chaparral and the sage brush, and thus hide until they could be protected by the darkness of the approaching night they discovered the Indians at a distance busily engaged in packing mules and horses with agency supplies. They were so occupied piling on the blankets and guns and stowing away the meat and flour that they did not see Dresser and the women and children until they had almost reached their goal. A wild yell, which came simultaneously from a score of throats, a mad rush and the discharge of firearms followed. Mrs. Meeker fell when struck by a ball, while Dresser, for whom the shot was most likely intended, bounded on and was lost in the dense growth.

The women could do nothing but place themselves at the mercy of the savages, who promised protection and security. However little confidence they may have had in this guarantee, no alternative but to accept and go along with them was left them. Their friends were all dead. They were helpless and in the hands of the slayers. Mrs. Meeker had scarcely fallen to the ground when a big buck, holding a gun in his hand, stood over her, his face illumined by a ghastly savage grin. "Me no hurt white squaw," he said; "Ute no hurt squaw, good squaw. Come to Douglass." Mrs. Meeker followed, limping after the red scoundrel, who had taken what money she had—some $30—and went to the camp of Douglass with him. She was then delivered over to the considerate care of that "good" chief, who rewarded her captor by giving him two silver dollar pieces which he had taken from the old lady. Mrs. Meeker has related in her own language what next transpired, and as in that is included a pathetic incident, which is all the more affecting as related by her, we repeat her words:

I told Douglass that I must have some blankets. He sent an Indian named Thompson to the burning building with me, and I got a hood, a shawl and one blanket. I handed around bedding,

Mrs. N. C. Meeker

etc., among the Indians, rather than have them destroyed. The Indians took them, and I afterward saw them in camp when I was suffering for the want of blankets to keep me warm. I went back to Douglass and said that I wanted my medicine and my 'spirit book.' I had doctored Douglass and his family. He said, 'Go'; so I went back a second time and got a large copy of *Pilgrim's Progress* and a box of medicines. The box was so heavy that an Indian refused to carry it. It was lost, but he took the book. When I got back to Douglass and told that chief the Indian had said that the medicine chest was too heavy to carry, Douglass looked disappointed and sorrowful, and asked—
'Couldn't you have split the box a little, so you could have brought part of it?'
In going back this last time I saw the body of my husband stretched out on the ground in front of the warehouse; all the clothing was gone but the shirt. The body was not mutilated. The arms were extended at the sides of the head. The face looked as peaceful and natural as in life, but blood was running from the mouth. I stooped to kiss him, but just as my lips were near his I saw an Indian standing stone still, looking at me, so I turned and walked away. Douglass afterward said that my husband was shot through the side of the head.

Mrs. Price surrendered to an Uncompahgre Ute, Cojoe by name, and Miss Josephine was made the captive of a subordinate chief or head man called Persune, whose name has become known to the outside world because of his gallant bearing toward the agent's daughter—"The pale white squaw who grieve much." When taken Miss Josephine was in charge of Mrs. Price's little girl May, while Mrs. Price still retained possession of Johnnie.

An incident worthy of note, to which doubtless the captives owe much of their fair treatment during the three weeks that succeeded this dreadful day, occurred a few minutes after the women and children had fallen into the hands of the barbarians. When Miss Josephine first went to the agency she was an object of much curious interest and of attention on the part of the Indians. Young, rosy-cheeked, bright, cheerful and vivacious, she charmed the savage eye and won the red man's heart. During her stay of over twelve months in their midst she was loved and wooed by fully a dozen braves, many of whom occupied first rank as chiefs. They made all kinds of offers to her, those that were married agreeing to put away their other wives, and those that were not swearing that their love and admiration for the white maiden should never be dimmed or diminished by affection for any other woman, wild and untutored or gentle and educated. One *moccasined* lover had hardly been sent away until another succeeded in his plea at the shrine of love. Douglass had himself become a victim to Miss Meeker's superior charms, and hesitated not to speak his admiration to the daughter of the agent. Persune, a younger and handsomer, and withal a better Indian, had also avowed his passion and his desire to possess "the white lily."

As was naturally to be expected there was a general anxiety to hold this treasure, now in the hands of the tribe. Persune had been alive to the situation, and while the other Indians were engaged in securing the agency goods, he was pursuing the fleeing charm, which he captured. He did not prove in all respects a gentle lover, and when in conducting his captive back to the Indian headquarters, he came to an irrigating canal, which had been constructed by the agent for the purpose of watering the valley, over which there was no means of crossing, he rudely dragged her through the water, which was quite deep, wetting her to the skin, so that when our heroine came up on the opposite bank, she was not in ballroom plight. Little May suffered the same indignity offered her protector, and also came out of the pool looking more like a clothes-line appendage than a piece of mortality.

Persune had scarcely more than emerged from this watery pathway than he came upon the great chief whom the whites call Douglass, but whose Indian cognomen is Quinkent, who no sooner discovered that Persune had made a captive of Miss Josephine, upon whom he had turned his own eye, than he entered an objection. It was plain to be seen that he had been drinking, for he swaggered and swore: Miss Josephine, who had seen only the better side of Douglass's character, was disposed to request him to take her, as she thought he would protect her. But second counsel with herself prevailed, and she decided to let the savages settle the matter among themselves, especially as she had little hope of influencing the result. She therefore held her tongue while the braves quarrelled over the possession of her. They came near to blows, and the young lady thought at one time that the day which had been so eventful and which had seen the spilling of so much of the blood of the white man, might yet see the letting of some of the extra supply of an Indian, or perhaps two. Little May clung close about her protector while the Indians disputed over the possession, seeming to assert that, let whomsoever might take her away, they two would not be parted.

Persune was not, however, in the least daunted by Douglass's *braggadocio*. He told him that the captive was his, and that he meant to retain possession of her, and after parleying for a while with the chief, and exchanging a few uncomplimentary epithets, alluding, among other things, to Douglass's connection with the Mountain Meadow massacre, he pushed the White River chief to one side and passed on with his captives, leaving Douglass to his own cogitations and chagrin.

The Indians told the women that they must now get ready for a long march, for they had a great way to go that night, to the squaws' camp, far away toward the Uncompahgre country. But this warning was almost unnecessary, as there were no preparations for them to make. Their clothing, except what they wore, had been burned with the other agency effects. The day had been warm, and as the ladies considered themselves out of the sight of all but "home folks," they had dressed themselves as scantily as they could for protection against the heat. They wore only their calico dresses, and neither shoes nor stockings. Thus they rendered themselves comfortable during the warmth of the day; but towards evening, in the mountains, when the sun begins to disappear, the air grows chill, and wraps and fires become comfortable. Darkness had come upon them while in this unprotected state, and the prospect of having to ride horseback during a long and cold night opened before them. They shuddered at the thought, and because of the cold. It was a case of mingled prospect and reality. The present was an indication of what the future, might be.

The Indians had finished their plundering and packing and were now ready to leave the agency and the agency ashes. The women were told to mount. Mrs. Meeker was set upon the bare back of a horse, behind Chief Douglass. Miss Josie was placed on a pony, and little May was lashed on behind her. She was provided with a saddle, but with no bridle, the Indians depending upon driving her horse as they desired it to go, rather than upon her guiding it. The Uncompahgre Ute who had captured Mrs. Price spread a blanket over the saddle of a pony and told her to mount. She crawled upon the animal's back, her baby boy was handed to her, and the Indian threw himself on behind. There were about twenty Indians in the party, all mounted, and with quite a number of annuity goods strapped on pack-mules. The Indians had attired themselves quite picturesquely before beginning the massacre, having assumed their feathers and their war-paint. These decorations they still retained.

The cavalcade started directly southward, taking the Indian trail to Grand River, which led gradually into the mountains. ' The sight was a peculiar one—as wild as weird and as weird as can well be imagined. The Indians and the women appeared in costumes which on the streets of any city would attract the gaze of all who might catch a glimpse of them. It would have made a fine picture, and the artist present would have lacked nothing to complete the view. Mountains, valleys, trees, streams, figures, Indian hilarity, female sorrow, the dark backgrounds of the agency and its recent scenes—all lighted by a full moon, which had just risen over the mountains to the east.

These were terrible times for the poor women. What thoughts must have crowded their brains! what phantoms taken shape! what pictures must have formed on the camera of the imagination! A day of terror such as mortal seldom experiences succeeded by a night among wild and drunken men, in fastnesses in the heart of the Rocky Mountains unexplored by men of their own race and colour. Having, as we may say, witnessed the massacre of husbands, fathers and friends; having been cooped up all day in a hole, for self-protection; having seen the buildings which had afforded them shelter crumble to the ground as the savage flames mounted to the skies; having almost been dragged over the dead bodies of their dead friends by their murderers, they were now, alone and without protection, trusting only to Providence for relief, in the hands of these barbarians, and were doomed to spend not only a night, but perhaps an eternity with them.

CHAPTER 11

Southward Bound

The trail was a well defined pathway, giving evidence of having been travelled for many a day by man and beast. It was tortuous and narrow, winding about on the hillsides and descending into the hollows, sometimes ascending an abrupt point and at others leading through a deep *cañon* with the mountains looming up, it seemed, well nigh to the skies, and cutting out all but the faintest shadows. But for the continual jabber of the Indians, the down-cast and sad-hearted women might have easily imagined a hundred armed warriors concealed behind as many pillars of stone and pine trees, ready to march stealthily forward and take possession of and murder them. The Indians seemed in excellent spirits, and, whether they marched up hill or down, laughed and talked continually, generally among themselves, but some times addressed their conversation to their captives.

Their naturally wild and uncouth characters were brought out in bolder relief by the use of whisky with which they seemed to be abundantly supplied, and which they used without stint. Each one carried a well filled bottle, which found its way to his mouth at short intervals. They had robbed the medicine stores at the agency of all the liquor to be obtained there, and were also evidently well supplied before they had begun their plundering. They drank and laughed continually. In fact, to use a common expression, they were gloriously drunk. But, as may well be imagined, their hilarity was in sad contrast to the feelings of the despairing women and frightened children. Relating her experience Mrs. Meeker says:

> Douglass's breath smelt strongly of whisky. He said:
> 'Your father dead; I had a father once; he too is dead. Agent no understand about the fight Indians make.'

The other Indians all took out bottles of whisky, which they held up between their eyes and the moon as they drank so as to see how much was left. Douglass as he rode along sang what seemed to be an obscene song to a pretty melody in slow measure. When he had finished he asked how I liked it. My limb ached so terribly that I could scarcely sit on the horse. Douglass held it a while; then he strapped it in a kind of a sling to his saddle.

I asked if I should see my daughter, Josephine. Douglass replied, 'Yes.'

As we rode a villainous looking Indian trotted alongside and slapped me on the shoulder and asked how I would like to be his squaw, and he made indecent proposals. Chief Douglass listened and laughed. He said the Indian was an Arapahoe, and I would kill Utes if I married an Arapahoe.

Mrs. Price relates that she was treated quite civilly by the Uncompahgre Indian who had made her a captive and who rode behind her. He pulled a watch out of his pocket and asked her if she recognised it. It proved to be a gold time-piece taken from Mr. Post, the agency clerk, and a valued family relic. The Indian, who evidently did not appreciate the value of the property, put the guard over Mrs. Price's head and strung it around her neck, saying it was her watch. She states that the road at times ascended such steep hills that she was almost unable to hold on, while Mrs. Meeker, who rode behind Douglass, was compelled to cling to him with all her strength to avoid falling off behind.

Persune early began to display towards Miss Josephine the gallantry which characterized him in all his dealings towards her. He rode alongside of her, driving his two pack-mules in front, and was not in the least rude or presuming. When she complained of thirst, he went to the river and brought her a drink in his hat. To illustrate the different degrees of politeness among savages, it may be related that Mrs. Price had also asked her Indian for some water, being also very thirsty. He gave it to her also out of his hat, but before handing it to her, drank himself. This Persune did not do.

The Indians travelled at a rapid trot for three or four hours and at last left the trail, and soon entered a small ravine, where they camped for perhaps half an hour, the prisoners being separated. Here the prisoners were told to dismount, and obeying instructions, they were carefully searched by the Indians, even to their shoes and stockings. They found on Mrs. Meeker's person a pocket-book, which was full of needles and a handkerchief. This last piece of property was taken by the ten-year-old son of Douglass, whose full name is Frederick Douglass. He is a boy ten years old, who had received special care at the hands of the women at the agency. He had been taught to read and to speak English to a degree.

His instructors were much encouraged at his progress, and thought, until they saw him in his real character, unrestrained by conventionalities, that he was a bright and shining contradiction of the prevailing opinion that the Indian could not be civilized. Now, however, that there were no restraints about him, and that his savage nature was at liberty to assert itself, it did not fail him. Like Mark Tapley, he came out strong. He not only stole Mrs. Meeker's handkerchief, but he abused her to the greatest extent possible with the words which had been taught him at the agency. He also taunted and jeered and poked fun at Miss Josephine and Mrs. Price, and teased and tormented the babies until they cried.

In doing these things the young Douglass only followed the example set by his illustrious sire and others of the tribe. Of all the Indians the house of Douglass seems to have proved on this occasion the most conspicuous. Miss Josephine had scarcely dismounted from her horse when this villain approached her in an indecent and threatening manner. She had lain down upon some blankets to take needed rest while stopping.

Chief Douglass addressed her as "white squaw," laughed at her, and then made her a speech, upbraiding her father, reciting his wrongs, and ending with a threat to kill her. He was greatly excited and used many gestures while speaking, representing what had been done— what he thought and felt—quite as much by actions as by words. He began with the story of his own grievances, which were many and trivial. He said the massacre (he had not yet heard of the Thornburgh fight, though they knew of his approach southward) occurred because Major Thornburgh, whom he knew not by name, but who was perfectly described, told the Indians that he was going to arrest the head chiefs, take them to Fort Steele and put them in the calaboose—perhaps hang them. He said Agent Meeker had written all the letters to the Denver papers and circulated wild reports about what the Indians would do, as set forth by the western press, and that he was responsible for all the hostility against the Indians among the whites in the west.

He manifested a perfect knowledge of what had been said in the papers, and quoted largely, almost word for word, from them.

He said, furthermore, that pictures of the agent and all his family, women and children, had been found on Thornburgh's body just before the attack on the agency, and the pictures were covered with blood, and showed marks of knives on different parts of the bodies. The throats were cut. The one of the agent had a bullet hole in his head. Josephine was represented in one of the pictures as shot through the breast. Douglass said Father Meeker had made these pictures, representing the prospective fate of his family, and sent them to Washington, to be used to influence the soldiers and hurry troops forward to fight the Indians.

This remarkable statement, strange as it may seem, was afterward repeated to the captives by a dozen different Indians, and the recital and the particulars were always the same.

While Douglass was telling this he stood in front of the captive girl with his gun, and his anger was dreadful. Then he shouldered his gun and walked up and down before her in the moonlight and imitated the *employés*, who had kept guard at the agency for three nights before the massacre. He mocked them, and sneered and laughed at them, and said he was "a heap big Indian." Then he sang English songs which he had heard the agency *employés* sing in their rooms. He sang the negro melody, "Swing Low, Sweet Chariot," and asked Josephine if she understood, which she easily did, because he had the words and tune perfectly committed. He said the agent had always been writing to Washington. He always saw him writing when he came to the agency. It was write, write, write all day, he said. Then he swore a fearful oath in English, and said if the soldiers had not come and threatened the Indians with Fort Steele and the calaboose and threatened to kill the other Indians at White River, the agent and *employés* would not have been massacred.

Then the brave chief, Douglass, who had eaten at the family table that very day, walked off a few feet, returned and placed his loaded gun to Josie's forehead three separate times, and asked her if she was going to run away.

She told him that she was not afraid of him nor of death, and should not run away.

When he found his repeated threats could not frighten her, all the other Indians turned on him and laughed at him, and made so much fun of him that he sneaked off and went over to frighten her mother.

CHIEF DOUGLASS.

She heard her cry "Oh!" and supposed that she thought some terrible fate had befallen her daughter, who shouted to her that she was not hurt; that she need not be afraid; that they were only trying to scare her. The night was still, but she heard no response.

What happened to Mrs. Meeker is related by her. She says:

> They talked indecently to us and made shameful proposals. They were drunk, and their conversation was loud with ribaldry. They even threatened me with death if I did not submit to their bestiality. Fortunately I escaped outrage, but had to submit to terrifying threats of violence and death. Douglass went through the burlesque of imitating the *employés* in keeping guard at the agency. He mocked the soldiers, walking up and down with a gun on his shoulder, and sang.
>
> As I lay on the ground, not knowing when I should be butchered, I thought of my young daughter Josephine, who was not far away, and wondered if she had already been slaughtered. My face was partly covered, but suddenly I heard Douglass's voice. I turned and saw Chief Douglass standing close by me, with the muzzle of his gun pointed directly at my face. I involuntarily cried out. Josephine heard me and her voice came out of the night, saying:
>
> 'I am all right, mamma , don't be afraid!'
>
> Douglass lowered his gun, raised it again and took aim. I said nothing and he walked away. An Indian standing near said:
>
> 'Douglass no hurt you. He only playing soldier.'"

After half an hour of this exhibition all hands took a drink around Josie's bed; then they saddled their horses, and Persune led the young lady's horse to her and knelt down on his hands and knees for her to mount from his back. He always did this, she says, and when he was absent his wife did it. She saw Persune do the same gallant act once for his squaw, but it was only once, and none of the other Indians did it at all for the other white women or their squaws.

They urged their horses forward and journeyed in the moonlight through to the Grand Mountains with the Indians talking in low tones among themselves, having greatly quieted down. The little three-year-old May Price, who was fastened behind Josephine, cried a few times, for she was cold and had had no supper, and her mother was away; but the child was generally quiet.

It was after midnight when they made the second halt in a deep and sombre *cañon*, with tremendous mountains towering on every side, where the squaws were camped. Mrs. Meeker was not allowed to come up where her daughter was. Douglass kept her with him half a mile further down the ravine. Mrs. Price was kept away from both of the other ladies, all being separated.

Mrs. Meeker's rough treatment, which continued during the entire captivity, began here. She says that when she reached the Ute women's camp, Douglass ordered her roughly to get off the horse. She was so lame and in such pain that she told him she could not move. He took her hand and pulled her off, and she fell on the ground, because she could not stand. An Indian and a squaw soon came and helped her up and led her to a tent. When she went to bed Douglass and his wife covered her with blankets, and she was more comfortable that night than at any other time during her captivity.

Relating her experiences of that night and the next morning, Mrs. Price says:

When we arrived at the camp that night, a squaw came and took my little boy from the horse and cried over him like a child. I dismounted and sat down in Persune's camp. I wasn't at all hungry, and when they offered me coffee, cold meat and bread I could not eat. After a while the squaw got over her weeping, when they talked and laughed. All I could understand was when they repeated the soldiers' names and counted what number of men they had killed at the agency. They said they had killed nine. At first they said ten, and I told them differently, as I thought Frank had escaped. They asked me how many, and seemed to accept my statement as correct.

They spread some blankets for me to lie on, but I could not sleep. The moon shone very brightly and everything looked ghastly. In the morning I went to Persune's tent and sat by the fire. I was cold, for I had nothing to wear except a calico dress. I sat there weeping—I could not help it—with my little boy in my arms. The squaws came around and talked and looked at me, and laughed and made fun of me. I didn't understand what they said, only occasionally a word. After a time some of the men came in and talked to the squaws, and looked at me and laughed.

Persune had plenty of blankets, which were stolen from the agency. He spread some for Miss Josephine's bed, and rolled up some for her

CAPTAIN JACK.

pillow and told her to retire. Then the squaws came and laughed, and grinned and gibbered in their own grim way. When she had lain down on the blankets two squaws, one old and one young, came to the bed, and sang and danced fantastically and joyously at her feet, piercing the wild mountain midnight air with their yells. The other Indians stood around, and when the women reached a certain part of their recitative they all broke into laughter. Toward the end of their song Persune gave each of them a newly stolen government blanket, which they took and then went away. The young lady relates that the strangeness and wild novelty of position kept her awake until toward morning, when she fell into a doze, and did not awake until the sun was shining over the mountains.

By this time the Indians were all astir, and Miss Josephine opened her eyes upon a wild and exciting scene. It was all understood when Douglass announced:

"Runner just come; Indians killed heap soldiers; Douglass go to front; gone five days."

It was evident that an Indian runner had followed close upon their heels the night before, bringing the news of the fight with Thornburgh, and that he had arrived early in the morning. The Indians were now off for the front, to assist their brethren in the resistance to the invasion of their country by the soldiers. The runner reported that Thornburgh had been killed and his troops forced to retreat to a point where they could be easily picked off by the Indians. The women were left with the squaws, and the bucks all took their leave for the scene of battle, Cojoe strapping a cartridge belt about him and going with the White River Utes.

At this juncture the story of the women becomes more interesting, as told in their own language, than in any other shape. Miss Josie says:

On Tuesday, after most of the men had left the camp, mother came up to see me, in company with a little Indian girl. On Wednesday, the next day, Johnson went over to Jack's camp and brought back Mrs. Price and her baby to live in his camp. He said he had made it all right with the other Utes.

We did not do anything but be around the various camps and listen to the talk of the squaws, whose husbands were away fighting the soldiers. On Wednesday and on other days one of Supanzisquait's three squaws put her hand on my shoulder and said:—

'Poor little girl, I feel so sorry; you have no father, and you are away off with the Utes so far from home.'

She cried all the time, and said her own little child had just died and her heart was sore. When Mrs. Price came into camp, another squaw took her baby, Johnny, into her arms and wept over him, and said in Ute that she felt very sorry for the captives.

Next day the squaws and the few Indians who were there packed up and moved the camp ten or twelve miles, into an exceedingly beautiful valley, with high mountains all around it. The grass was two feet high, and a stream of pure soft water ran through the valley. The water was so cold I could hardly drink it.

Every night the Indians, some of whom had come back from the soldiers, had councils. Mr. Brady had just come up from the Uncompahgre Agency with a message from Chief Ouray, for the Indians to stop fighting the soldiers. He had delivered the message, and this was why so many came back.

On Sunday, most of them were in damp. They said they had the soldiers hemmed in a *cañon*, and were merely guarding them. Persune came back, wearing a pair of soldier's blue pantaloons, with yellow stripes on the legs. He took them off and gave them to me for a pillow. His legs were protected with leggings, arid he did not need them. I asked the Indians before Brady came where the soldiers were. They replied that they were "still in that cellar," and the Indians were killing their ponies when they went for water in the night. They said:—

'Indian stay on mountains and see white soldiers; soldiers no see Indian; white soldier not know how to fight.'

Mrs. Price, says:

About an hour after supper of the day the Indians left, an old squaw ordered me to go with her to another tent to sleep, so I went to Henry Jim's tent, where I sat down. They had no fire, but soon made one, and the squaws crowded around. Henry asked me a few questions. He said he felt very bad for me. He said he told the Utes not to murder the people at the agency. He had been assisting the issuing clerk and acted as interpreter. He said they were friendly and he liked them very much. He said the Utes told him he was nothing but a little boy for refusing to kill the white men at the agency, but when they called him a boy he said it was too much for him.

He had no more to say after that. He asked me if I was going to stay all night in his tent. I said the squaw had brought me over there to sleep. He said, 'All right; you stay here all night.' So his squaw made me a very nice bed of about ten blankets. I went to bed and she tucked me in quite nicely. I slept well, got up, washed myself, combed my hair and felt pretty well. Henry's squaw cooked breakfast. She made bread and prepared some coffee and fried venison, and there was another squaw who brought in some fried potatoes.

I ate breakfast with my little boy in my arms, and presently Chief Johnson came in, looking very angry and troubled. He said gruffly, 'Hallo, woman!' and shook hands. He sat down and presently three more Utes came in. Johnson got out his pipe and they all had a smoke around, and they talked about the soldiers and their big battle.

Henry said to me: 'You go now with Johnson to see your little girl, who is with Josephine.' So I mounted the horse behind Chief Johnson and rode about five miles, and when I came up to Douglass's camp I first saw Mrs. Meeker, and I went up to her, shook hands and kissed her, and felt very badly for her. She said:

'Don't make any fuss.'

Josephine and my little girl had been to a brook to get a drink. We sat down and had a nice talk until the squaws came and told me I must go to Johnson's tent and the little girl to Persune's. Miss Josie went down to Johnson's tent, where they put down Mrs. Meeker's comforter for me to sit down on, and asked if I was hungry. I told them yes, and they went to work and cooked some dinner for me.

The next day we moved from that place to another camp. It was a very nice place, with grass two feet high, a nice brook of clear, cool water flowing through it. The Indians had killed many soldiers and were prancing around in their coats and hats, putting on airs and imitating soldiers, and making fun of them while going through a burlesque drill, and making believe they were the greatest warriors in the west.

They took a great fancy to my little child and wanted to keep him. They crept into the tent after him, and when they found they could not steal him they offered three ponies for him.

MRS. PRICE AND HER BABIES

In the afternoon, about two o'clock, they cut a lot of sage brush, piled it up and spread over it the clothes they had stolen from the soldiers. Four of the Indians then began to dance around them, and at intervals fell on their knees before them and thrust their knives into them and went through a mimic massacre of soldiers. Other Utes kept joining the party that was dancing until a ring was made as big as a good sized house. They would first run away, then turn and dance back the other way, yelling and hollowing like frescoed devils. They had war suits, fur caps with eagle feathers, and they looked strangely hideous. They wanted Miss Josie and me to dance with them. We told them we could not. 'We no *sabe* dance.'

That afternoon Mrs. Meeker came over and we had an old-fashioned talk. She told us her troubles. They had threatened to stab her with knives, she said. Charley, Chief Douglass's son-in-law, soon came around in a very bad humour, and as he could speak good English we didn't dare to talk much after he appeared. Mrs. Meeker said she felt as though she might be killed any night; that they treated her very meanly. Josephine seemed downhearted, though she was plucky. I tried to cheer her all I could.

The Indians would not let us go alone any distance from the camp. They asked me if I had any money, and I told them I did not, as it was all burned. We asked them where the soldiers were, and they said they were down in that cellar, meaning the entrenchments. They said the Indians would lay around on the mountains and kill the soldiers' horses. The soldiers would not appear at all in the day time. At night they would slip out, only to be shot by the Indians.

They threatened if I attempted to run away they would shoot me. Johnson put a gun to my forehead and told me he would kill me. I said:

'Shoot away. I don't care if I die; shoot if you want to.'

He laughed then, and would say: 'Brave squaw; good squaw; no scare.'

They also said Josephine would very soon die, as she drank no coffee and ate very little. I told them it was the same at the agency, that she ate little and drank no coffee. They talked it over among them selves and said no more about it. They made fun of Mrs. Meeker, and said 'maybe the Utes will kill her.' I said to them: 'No, don't you kill my mother; I heap like her.' 'All right,' they would say. 'Pretty good mother; pretty good mother.' Cojoe pointed his gun at me and threatened to kill me many times.

The Indians held considerable conversation with each other in regard to the massacre and tried to get information from us. They told various stories how the fight occurred and who were concerned in it. From all that I heard of their talk I think Antelope or Pauviets shot the agent. Chief Johnson said he shot Thornburgh in the forehead three times with his pistol, and then got off his pony and he went to him and pounded him in the head and smashed his skull all in. They took some of his clothes off, but I did not see any of them worn in camp. The Indians Ebenezer, Douglass, Persune, Jim Johnson and Charley Johnson were at the agency massacre. Jack was not there. He was fighting the soldiers. Johnson's brother Iata was killed by Frank Dresser. Washington was on the ground. They all had guns and helped to shoot. Josephine said she saw an Indian named Creep there. I did not see any of the bodies at the agency. I only heard the firing and saw the Indians shooting toward the buildings where the men were working.

The Utes said they were going to kill all the soldiers, and that the women should always live in the Utes' camp, excepting Mrs. Meeker. Douglass said she could go home by and by, when she would perhaps see Frank Dresser, who, the Indians thought, had escaped. They made me do more drudgery than they did Josephine. They made her cook and made me carry water. They told me to saddle the pony, and I told them I didn't know how.

Mrs. Meeker's story covers many points of interest not touched upon by either her daughter or Mrs. Price, and we reproduce it also. She says:

Douglass's squaw treated me very well for one or two days; then she began to ill-use me, and gave me nothing to eat for one day. While Douglass was gone his son-in-law told me frightful stories. He said the Indians 'no shoot' me, but would stab me to death with knives. One squaw went through the pantomime of roasting me alive—at least I so understood it. Josephine told me that it was only done to torment me. If Douglass had got killed,

I would probably have been punished. A row of knives was prepared, with scabbards, and placed in the tent for use. Then Douglass's son-in-law, Johnson, came to me and asked if I had seen the knives being fixed all day. I said 'Yes.' He replied that 'Indians perhaps stab' me and 'no shoot' me. 'You say Douglass your friend; we see Douglass when come back from soldiers.'

Many of the squaws looked very sorrowful, as if some great calamity were about to happen; others were not kind to me, and Freddie Douglass, the chief's son, whom I had taken into my house at the agency, and washed and taught and doctored and nursed and made healthy, came to me in my captivity and mocked me worse than all the rest. The Douglass blood was in him, and he was bad. He said I was a bad squaw and an old white squaw. He tried to steal the old wildcat skin that I slept on, and he stole my handkerchief while I was asleep and jeered me during my imprisonment.

Douglass returned from fighting the soldiers on Saturday night. On the next day his wife went back to the agency for the cabbages raised by the cultivation the Indians professed so much to despise. Douglass was morose and sullen, and had little to say. He did not seem to be satisfied with the military situation, but thought the Indians would annihilate the soldiers. Large numbers of head men and captains came to consult Douglass. They were in and out most of the night, making speeches and discussing things in general, as though the fate of the universe depended on their decision. Douglass often asked us where the agent was. I said that I did not know. Douglass rejoined that neither did he know. Mrs. Douglass treated me spitefully, and her chief was not much better, though he gave me enough to eat. When he was gone, very little was cooked."

On Sunday night Jack came to camp and made a big speech, as also did Johnson. They said more troops were coming, and they recited what orders they said had been brought from Chief Ouray. They were in great commotion, and did not know what to do. They talked all night, and the next morning they struck half their tents and put them up again. Part were for going away, part for staying, and being undecided they remained. Jack's men were all day coming up into camp, and all left on Tuesday morning before daylight for Grand River and they had a long ride. The cavalcade was fully two miles long. The wind blew a hurricane, and the dust was so thick that Miss Josephine says she could not see ten feet back on the line, and she could write her name on her hand in the dust. Most of the Indians had had no breakfast, and they travelled all day without food or water.

Mrs. Meeker says:

It was a very long and terrible journey that I made that day. I rode a pony with neither saddle nor bridle nor stirrups. There was only a tent cloth strapped on the horse's back, and an old halter to guide him with. It was the most distressing experience of my life. Not a single halt was made, and my pain was so great that the cold drops stood on my forehead. I could only cling to the pony by riding astride. We travelled rapidly, over mountains so steep that one would find difficulty in walking over them on foot. The dust was suffocating, and I had neither water nor dinner. Josephine and Mrs. Price rode ahead. One of the mountains was so steep that, after making part of the ascent, Douglass's party had to turn back and go around it. This incident shows what hardships delicate women on bare-back horses had to endure. We reached a camping ground half an hour after dark and pitched our tents in the valley. I was so faint that I could not get off the horse nor move until a kind woman assisted me to the ground. I was too ill and exhausted to eat, and I went to bed without any supper.

The camp that night was in the sage brush. The following morning (Wednesday) they moved five miles down the river.

CHAPTER 12

Marching on to the Final Camping Place

The Indians, Johnson apparently in charge, remained on Grand River with their captives until Saturday. While there Miss Josephine sent a note to the Uintah Agency in Utah by Uintah Utes, who were with the hostiles, requesting that it be forwarded. It read as follows:

> Grand River, 40 to 50 Miles from Agency,
> Oct. 10, 1879.
>
> To Uintah Agent:
> I send this by one of your Indians. If you get it do all in your power to liberate us as soon as possible. I do not think they will let us go of their own accord. You will do me a great service to inform Mary Meeker, at Greeley, Col., that we are well and may get home some time.
>
> Yours, etc.,
>
> Josephine Meeker,
> United States Indian Agent's daughter.

The note was written with a lead pencil on the back of a piece of paper which had formerly done service as a dry goods label. It reached Washington on the 30th of October, after the captives were liberated, and was not then of the service it might have been under different circumstances.

The mountains were very high, and the Indians were on the peaks with glasses watching the soldiers. They said they could look down on the site of the agency. Johnson had field glasses and all day he was watching the soldiers, and would only come down to his supper. The Indians took turns watching during the night, and during the day

106

they covered the hills and watched the soldiers through their glasses. Runners came in with foaming steeds constantly. On Saturday morning the programme was for twenty Utes to go back to White River, scout around on the mountains and watch the soldiers; but just as they were about to depart there was a terrible commotion, for some of the scouts on the mountains had discovered the troops, ten or fifteen miles south of the agency, advancing toward the camp.

The Indians ran in every direction, the horses became excited, and for a time hardly a pony could be approached. Johnson flies into a passion when there is danger. This time his horses kicked and confusion was supreme. Johnson seized a whip and laid it over the shoulders of his youngest squaw, named Cooz. He pulled her hair and renewed the lash until she cried and screamed. He then went to help his other squaw, Susan, Chief Ouray's sister, pack up. They put Mrs. Price and her baby on one horse, and strapped little May in a blanket behind Josephine. Johnson was very mad and pointed his gun at Mrs. Price and Miss Josephine. Mrs. Price told him to shoot away, and asked him to shoot her in the forehead. He said:

"No, good squaw; no scare."

They then started for another camping place south of the Grand River.

The next day was Sunday, and the camp and Miss Josephine were again moved twenty-five miles south to a point on Grand River; but Mrs. Meeker and Mrs. Price did not come up for three or four days. The rain set in and continued two days and three nights. Miss Josie did not suffer, for she was in camp, but the other ladies and the baby, who were kept on the road, were soaked each day. Johnson, who had Mrs. Price, went beyond the camp in which Miss Meeker was left, and all the other Indians behind camped with Johnson.

Johnson's oldest wife is the sister of Chief Ouray, and he was kinder than the others. His wife cried over the captives and made the children shoes.

The Indians said they would stay at their camp, and if the soldiers advanced, they would get them in a says and kill them all. They said that neither American soldiers nor American horses understood the country. The Utes were now close to the Uncompahgre district, and could not retreat much farther. Colorow made a big speech, and advised the Indians to go no farther south. However, they were removed one day's ride to Plateau Creek, a little stream emptying into Grand River from the south. Eight miles more travel on two other days

Doctor Johnson.

brought them to the camping ground where General Adams found them. This was near to Plateau Creek, but high up, and not far from the snowy range.

After this last place was reached, Douglass permitted Josephine to see her mother every day, and the long hours were more endurable. Mrs. Meeker says:

The courage of the brave girl and her words of hope cheered me very much. My life would not have been safe had it not been for her influence with the Indians. She could speak some of their language, and she made them cease terrifying me with their horrible threats and indecent stories. She finally forced Douglass to give me a saddle, so that in the last days of journeying I had something besides a bareback horse to ride upon. It gave me great joy on one of the evenings of those terrible first days to have her, as we passed each other in the moonlight, sing out cheerily:

'Keep up good courage, mother; I am all right; we shall not be killed.'

The last evenings of the stay among the red devils were devoted to songs and merry making by those who were not away on the mountains watching the soldiers. Mrs. Price joined in some of the choruses, because it helped the captives and made the Indians more lenient. They told a great variety of stories and cracked jokes on each other and on the white men. They had dances and medicine festivals. Speaking of these trying times Mrs. Price says:

In regard to my days of captivity I can only say the Indians were at times lively and joked with us, so that I was forced to laugh a good many times at their strange humour when I did not feel like it. It seemed to please them very much. They would say 'Buena momets' (good woman). When Josephine came in they would say she was cross. She was very much grieved, and when her blood was up she talked to them in a lively strain and made them treat Mrs. Meeker better. After Johnson and Mrs. Meeker had talked together about the agent, Mrs. Meeker came to Johnson's to stay. He treated her with great care. Previously she was not welcomed. The meanest thing they did to the poor little woman was to frighten her with their knives and horrible grimaces and bad stories. They tried to scare us all out of our wits.

The children also took part in their festivities and sang as gleefully and loudly as if real *papooses*, thus increasing their favour with the Utes, until before the captives left the savages made Mrs. Price an offer of ten ponies for them.

The singing of the medicine song is always resorted to when an Indian is sick, and Miss Josephine was favoured with several opportunities to witness these ceremonies.

As a usual thing no whites are admitted to the tents while these songs are in progress, but she being considered one of Persune's family, was allowed to remain. When Persune's child was sick his family asked Josephine to sing with them, which she did. The Medicine Man kneels close to the sufferers, with his back to the spectators, while he sings in a series of high-keyed grunts, gradually reaching a lower and solemn tone. The family join, and at intervals he howls so loudly that one can hear him a mile; then his voice dies away and only a gurgling sound is heard, as if his throat were full of water. The child lies nearly stripped. The doctor presses his lips against the breast of the sufferer and repeats the gurgling sound. He sings a few minutes more, and then all turn around and smoke and laugh and talk. Sometimes the ceremony is repeated all night. Miss Josie assisted at two of these medicine festivals. Mrs. Price's boy became expert at singing Ute songs, and the children sang to each other on the journey home. The sick-bed ceremonies were very strange, and Miss Meeker says weird, and more interesting than anything she saw in all her captivity of twenty-three days.

Frequent war dances were also witnessed. One of their favourite amusements was to put on a negro soldier's cap, a short coat and blue pantaloons, and imitate the negroes in speech and walk. The captives could not help laughing because they were so accurate in their personations. On Sunday they made a pile of sagebrush as large as a washstand, and put soldiers' clothes and a hat on the pile; then they danced a war dance and sang as they waltzed around it. They were in their best clothes, with plumes and fur dancing caps, made of skunk skins and grizzly bear skins, with ornaments of eagle feathers. Two or three began the dance, and others joined, until a ring as large as a house was formed. There were some squaws, and all had knives. They charged on the pile of coats with their knives and pretended that they would burn the brush. They became almost insane with frenzy and excitement. The dance lasted from two o'clock until sundown.

In these war dances, the grotesque and horrible form a dreadful accompaniment, which even to a savage mind can be excused only by

INDIAN WAR DANCE

the dread uncertainty of the war to follow the uncouth ceremony. The devil is particularly materialized for the occasion, and the enemies of the tribe turned over to his domain, while the wild bull of the happy hunting grounds is propitiated, in the hope that his prototypes in the opposing camp will become the loot of the victors.

Notwithstanding these hilarities, however, the Indians were troubled and anxious about the troops. Runners were constantly coming and going. The least rumour or movement of the soldiers threw the Indians into a flutter. Chief Douglass began to realise the peril of the situation. Colorow advised them to go no farther south, though the troops were moving down from the north. "They had better fight," he said, "and defend their camps, than retreat." Chief Ouray, the friend of the whites, did not want the White River Utes on his domain. Douglass spoke of the agency as gone forever. He said it would have to be built up again. The Indians had lost all, and with a sigh he exclaimed:

"Douglass a heap poor man now."

When he had time he fell to abusing the agent, and said that if he had kept the troops away, there would have been no war.

The Indians, when in camp, spent their time moulding bullets from lead which they carried, singing, drinking, dancing, holding councils to discuss the state of affairs, and in referring to the scenes of the few preceding days. They told over and over again the story of the White River massacre, alleging gross provocation suffered from Meeker, the delay of the government in paying them what it owed, and the advance of the troops, as excuses. They said that Colonel Thornburgh and many of his soldiers were intoxicated at the time of the battle on Milk Creek. They also denied mutilating the bodies of their victims. They repeated and re-repeated the assertion that Agent Meeker was a bad man; that he lied about them, and would not issue supplies to them unless they would work; and that when they refused to work, he threatened to bind them with handcuffs and chains and hang them.

They said that he told them that Thornburgh had chains with him, and that upon his arrival he would help to bind and hang them. (This probably accounts for their binding Meeker's body, as at the agency, where the body lay, when first seen a chain was found around his neck.) They said that they interviewed Thornburgh at Bear River and on Williams' Fork before the fight on Milk River, when he appeared haughty and would not afford them any explanation or satisfaction, saying that he was a big warrior, too, and would go to the agency with his whole command, and not a few men only, as they asked him to do, and that he was their best friend when fighting them; that they were his best friends when fighting him, although they might kill him; and that, while so talking, he held a loaded carbine ready in his hands and seemed to want to fight; that thereupon, they determined to resist his march through the *cañon*, and stationed themselves on Milk River, at the mouth of the *cañon*, to await his arrival and show their determination.

Colonel Thornburgh persisted in pursuing his march toward the agency, and the fight ensued September 29th on Milk River, Colonel Thornburgh being one of the first to fall, the Indians losing twenty men in the first day's fight and thirty-four in all during the irregular fight of six days with Thornburgh's command, two of the thirty-four being killed in the skirmish with Merritt's men Sunday morning, October 5th, upon the arrival of the relief column.

The arrangements for a fight with Merritt's command they said were most complete. Two hundred Arapahoes, according to account, had joined Jack, and many others from the neighbouring tribes, and had it not been for the timely arrival of Chief Ouray's order to cease fighting the name of Merritt and his command would have passed into history by the side of Custer, with the same epitaph—"Annihilated by Indians."

They seemed especially to despise Agent Meeker and the efforts which had been made to improve and civilize them. One day a squaw said to Mrs. Meeker:

"What could you expect? The Indians had to kill the whites, because neither they nor the agent would do as the Utes told them to do."

Many of the Indians during those times made confessions which may well be used to their detriment in the investigation now in progress. Chief Johnson, while speaking of the battle with the troops, avowed himself to be the one who fired the shot which killed Colonel Thornburgh, and Mrs. Price in relating her experience says:

While Douglass was drunk he told me a lot of things that he don't know of now. If he had ever remembered, he would have killed me. He arranged the whole thing, and the soldiers coming has made him afraid, and he is trying to get out of it now. He's the smartest and meanest of them all.

They generally agreed that Jack led the fight at Milk River, while Douglass conducted the massacre at the agency.

Washington expressed himself freely. "Meeker heap fool," he said speaking of the agent. "Me no likum work. Make Washington heap tired. Me shoot; me no work. Me killum black tail." Washington did not like Ouray, and was not especially friendly towards Douglass. He said that Ouray had sold Indian land and put the money which he had received for it into his own pocket. In fact Washington did not seem to like any Indian except himself. He was a good Ute—liked the white man, never troubled the whites, wouldn't lie or steal, and so on. After a eulogy on his virtues he took carefully from his vest pocket a soiled envelope, from which he took a piece of legal cap paper, which he handed to his white auditors with much satisfaction of manner. It was a "character" and read about as follows:

The bearer, George Washington, is a good Ute. He will not steal the white man's horses, nor anything else from the white man.

The signature was a scrawl, which meant nothing. When the paper was returned to him he put it away as carefully as if it had been his last dollar bill and he a thousand miles from home. It is needless to add that Washington is a sneak and a scoundrel.

While remaining here, awaiting the arrival of General Adams on his mission of mercy, it will not be out of place to give the reader the tradition of the Indians in regard to the geological history of their country, the scene of the tradition being laid very near where the Indians were then encamped. This legend is to the effect that the forefathers of the tribe, long years ago, lived near a vast warm lake northeast of the Big River; that the country was warm, full of big trees and big deer and big oxen with white horns; that big fishes and snakes as long as an hundred lodge poles abounded in this lake; that one day all the big oxen began to roar together, and that they raised such a steam from their nostrils that the earth reeled and the sun was obscured; that suddenly the lake fell, and continued falling for three moons, and then became so much reduced that they knew it not any more, but that the big lake they found had been drained away to the south, and that its warm water had gone out through the mountains, the present *cañon* of Green River and of the Big River (the Colorado); and that his old bed in the Toom-pin-to-weep, as they call the stream, is where the lake waters were drained.

They also say that the story goes on that all the big deer and the big oxen with white horns strayed away east ward, and all perished in the mountains from cold or by the arrows of the Ute hunters; that soon after a big flood formed Grand River Cañon, and after this flood came a small race of people who had skin canoes, and who brought seed corn of a small kind, called in Spanish *chiquito maze*; that these people were almost white, and that they taught the Utes how to make good spears and bows and earthenware; that they built stone houses in the cliffs, and cultivated pumpkins, corn and beans; that they had silver and gold in abundance, and iron tools that they had obtained in the mountains to the northeast; that after wards, from the northwest, came big red Indians over to this country and killed and drove off the little people, who finally all went south, as we'll as the big red men, who are the Apaches, Navajoes and Kiowas.

They also say that the big oxen with white horns, the *grande lagarios* (probably alligators), were found down among the Apache and Navajo Indians, but that by and by the country became dryer and colder, and the Utes only were left on the Big River and its branches; that melted rocks were poured out everywhere and left the country desolate, and that the little people had told their forefathers that where they came from were big waters, and in these waters were men with bodies like a fish. They say that in this old river bed is plenty of gold, but that it is sure death for anyone to go into the *cañon* to get it.

And while we are speaking of the formation of the land it will not be out of place to refer to it now, especially as there are good grounds for hoping that it will now be opened to settlement by the removal of the Indians. Speaking of the nation from an agricultural point of view, General Adams says:

> It is good for nothing. There is room for two or three good cattle ranches, but nothing else. The elevation is 8,500 feet, and nothing but potatoes will grow there. Out of the 12,000,000 acres in the entire reservation, perhaps 25,000 in the Uncompahgre valley could be cultivated. I rode one hundred miles along the Grand River and did not find in the whole distance feed for my horse. One year the government supported a farmer on the reservation at $60 a month. Besides this he had his living. He raised as the result of this year's work twelve potatoes, three heads of lettuce and two bunches of radishes. Except the Uncompahgre Valley there is no country worth anything for farming.

The Uncompahgre Valley of which General Adams speaks is a lovely strip of land running through the southern portion of the res-

115

ervation. Settlers have already squatted upon portions of it, which yield splendid crops of all cereals, corn, garden vegetables, including potatoes, turnips, etc. This river empties into the Grand, which is also skirted by pretty valleys as are many of the other creeks and rivers. In Powell Bottom, on White River, Agent Meeker was making excellent progress in growing wheat and potatoes. There are doubtless many valleys besides the Uncompahgre which would produce well; and as for the grazing, it is unexcelled. The cattle on Bear River are always in better condition than those on the plains, and the agency herd at White River were in excellent shape when the massacre began. There is no conjecture concerning the existence of mineral wealth. Iron ore and splendid coal were found in the greatest abundance near White River Agency. In deed Mr. Meeker opened up five or six coal mines within a few miles of his location. On Anthracite Creek, a branch of the North Fork of the Gunnison River, on the reservation, Mr. Richard Irwin has opened up a bed of anthracite coal which is unexcelled anywhere in the world. The best coking coal in the west is found here.

In this same neighbourhood placer gold has been found in large quantities, and most miners believe that quartz lodes of both gold and silver will be found whenever they shall be afforded an opportunity to search for them.

Climatically the country is during most seasons of the year more pleasant than that on the east side of the mountains.

The scenery is beautiful. Anyone who has visited the wonderful land which lies *"over the range"* knows how impossible it is to put on paper a description which will give the reader anything like a realising conception of the country. The immense height of the hills and loftier crags and peaks, the seemingly immeasurable depth of chasms and *cañons*, the wonderful expansion of distances, the colour and character and density of brush and timber, all unite in forming a veritable *terra incognita* totally unlike anything which lies beyond the Missouri River. The fantastical contortions of the earth's surface are chiefly due to volcanic action, of which evidences appear at every turn. Great cliffs of lava ridge the parks, and the same substance is found intruded between *strata* of other rock, split asunder by the convulsions which made these mountains untold centuries ago, and he who is venturesome enough to climb the giddy heights will every now and then come upon the well defined crater of an extinct volcano.

Fossils—unmistakable seashells—have been dug from heights ten or eleven thousand feet above tidewater, unquestionably put there by the upheaval which lifted these lofty ranges from depths below the sea. From two hundred miles east from the White River Agency, extending north into the British possessions, south far down into Mexico and westward almost to the Pacific, a net work of ranges, whose peaks tower from ten to fifteen thousand feet above sea level—from two to six or seven thousand feet above the rapid rivers which wind through the narrow valleys between them—are the Rocky Mountains. Although the great "divide" which parts the waters flowing into the two great oceans is termed "the Snowy Range," it is not proper to speak of the Rockys as a "range" in the sense that the term may be applied to the Green Mountains or the Alleghanies. They are rather a succession of interwoven ranges, extending north and south the whole length of the Continent, and almost a thousand miles from east to west.

It may be doubted if the fiftieth part of the territory included within their boundaries is capable of tillage, to say nothing of climatic difficulties. But the whole region abounds with the best imaginable hiding places for thousands of fugitives, and almost insurmountable obstacles to invaders. The most available passes between the peaks are of some eleven thousand feet elevation, while many others, which must be crossed to reach certain districts, are much higher; and all of them impassable for six or seven months of the year except on snow shoes. As the sun advances higher and higher north of the Equator these great snow barriers are gradually dissolved, and, running down the steep declivities in thousands of mountain rivulets, are gathered in the valleys in foaming torrents, tearing through numberless inaccessible *cañons* unbridged and unfordable, except at rare intervals.

A maze of trails webs the whole region, perplexing and misleading the stranger, but as familiar to the roving aborigines as the streets of New York to the native *gamin*, who roams all over the island without ever looking at the signs at street corners, which he could not read if he did. There is hardly any level ground, scarcely one acre in a hundred. The whole country is up and down, with such steep ascents and sharp declivities as cannot well be imagined by those who have not seen them.

Short, nutritious, wild mountain grasses grow in profusion in the valleys and on the hills, and even cover the lofty mountain tops, far above timber line, wherever they happen not to be naked rock. These grasses, unlike those of lesser altitudes, cure on the ground, and after their life goes out retain the properties of hay. Subsistence for animals is, therefore, abundant so long as it is not covered with snow or the country be not burned over; in that case the transportation of forage becomes one of the most serious and expensive obstacles to invasion.

But this wonderful and inaccessible country—so full of peril and hardship to the white man—is the home of the Indian. He has climbed those crags from childhood and knows every trail and ford. He has learned to measure those heights and distances with eyes which can see an approaching enemy miles and miles away, while the observation is unsuspected and the signals which telegraph his coming from peak to peak are little dreamed of. He is as familiar with every nook and corner of this rough, wild maze for hundreds of miles in every direction from his agency as any farmer's boy of sporting proclivities is with the woods and glens and thickets which lie within ten miles of his paternal acres. The light air has no depressing influence upon his powers and endurance, for he has run and leaped and climbed and hunted in it all his life.

He does not suffer from the cold and snow, for he has learned to endure and protect himself against them winter after winter. He clothes himself in furs, and goes forth fearlessly in the roughest weather, or wraps himself in buffalo or bear skins and sleeps warm and comfortable when the mercury is out of sight. Practice has taught him to go for days without eating, and if it is not convenient to cook the game he lives on, he will take it raw with equal relish. For all practical purposes there is no limit to the number of his ponies, strong of limb and sure-footed, fleet as the wind, tough and hardy as their master, accustomed to carry him one hundred miles in a day whenever called upon, to climb those steeps and swim those torrents, and to subsist and grow fat on mountain grass, summer and winter, pawing, when necessary, through the snow to find it.

On Monday night the captives were told that a white man, whom they called Washington, and who proved to be General Adams, would come soon. At last an Uncompahgre Ute came from Chief Ouray and spoke very kindly, and as he sat by the fire, said:

"Tomorrow five white men coming and some Indians."

Among them would be "Chicago man Sherman, a great big peace man." General Adams and the Indians were going to have a talk and the captives would go home. The Uncompahgre said that a wagon would be waiting at a certain place below the plateau.

Relating the arrival of the Adams party, Miss Josephine says:

GENERAL ADAMS

The next day, about eleven o'clock, while I was sewing in Persune's tent, his boy, about twelve years old, came in, picked up a buffalo robe and wanted me to go to bed. I told him I was not sleepy. Then a squaw came and hung a blanket before the door, and spread out both hands to keep the blanket down, so I could not push it away; but I looked over the top and saw General Adams and party outside on horses.

The squaw's movements attracted their attention, and they came up close. I pushed the squaw aside and walked out to meet them. They asked my name and dismounted; said they had come to take us back, if we cared to go. I showed them the tent where mother and Mrs. Price were stopping, and the general went down, but they were not in; for, meanwhile, Johnson had gone to where they were washing, on Plateau Creek, and told them that a council was to be held, and that they must not come up until it was over. Dinner was sent to the ladies, and they were ordered to stay there. About four o'clock, when the council ended, General Adams ordered them to be brought to him, which was done, and once more we were all together in the hands of our friends.

We now quote Mrs. Meeker:

When I first saw General Adams I could not say a word, my emotion was so great. We had borne insults and threats of death, mockery and ridicule, and not one of us had shed a tear, but the sight of General Adams, Captain Cline, Mr. Sherman and their men was too much for me. My gratitude was greater than my speech. We owe much to the wife of Johnson. She is Ouray's sister, and, like him, she has a kind heart. Ouray had ordered us to be well treated and that we should be allowed to go home.

The council was a stormy one. Various opinions prevailed. The war party wanted us held until peace should be made between the Indians and the government. They wanted to set us against the guilty murderers, so as to save them through us. After a few hours of violent speeches, Mrs. Johnson burst into the lodge, in a magnificent wrap, and demanded that the captives should be set free, war or no war. Her brother Ouray had so ordered, and she took the assembly by storm. She told the pathetic story of the captives, and advised the Indians to do as Ouray requested and trust to the mercy of the government. General Adams said he must have a decision at once, or he would have to leave. That settled it, and we were set free.

Next morning, when we were about to start for the wagon, which was a day's journey to the south, Chief Johnson, who was slightly cool toward us, threw out a poor saddle for me to ride upon. His wife Susan caught sight of it and was furious. She flung it away and went to a pile of saddles and picked out the best one in the lot. She found a good blanket, and gave both to me. Then she turned to her chief and poured out her contempt with such effect that he was glad to sneak away.

So long as I remember the tears which this good woman shed over the children, the words of sympathy which she gave, the kindness that she continually showed to us, I shall never cease to respect her and to bless the goodness of her brother, Ouray, the Spanish-speaking chief of the south. I trust all the good people will remember them.

All the ladies agree that Susan was uniformly kind and pleasant. Mrs. Price says:

Johnson's wife was very kind. She treated me just like a mother, though sometimes when tired she would order me to get water. She treated my little girl very kindly, made *moccasins* for her, and she grieved over her and my boy as if they were her own. She said the Utes had killed the child's papa; 'Utes no good.' She was for peace. She was Chief Ouray's sister, and Ouray was friendly to the whites, and had sent messages to her to see that the whites were not abused and should be returned soon.

In this connection a story coming from the lips of Major Whitely, who was for several years agent at White River, will be found of great interest. The major relates that while on his way to the Hot Sulphur Springs, in Middle Park, he was overtaken by a messenger from Governor Evans, who informed him of the rescue of a Ute squaw from the Arapahoes and Cheyennes by the officers of the United States Army at Fort Collins. These Indians had captured this squaw in some of their raids, and, while encamped near the mouth of the Cache La Poudre, had determined to burn her at the stake. The commanding officer at Fort Collins hearing of this, took a detachment of troops, and by alternate threats and promises obtained her release, after she had already been tied to the stake and the fires lighted. This squaw was forwarded to Major Whitely, and after her arrival at Hot Springs was sent by him to her people, being accompanied by U. M. Curtis, the major's interpreter, and delivered to them after a journey across the western portion of Colorado into the border of Utah, to the camp of the Indians on the Snake River, where she was received with every demonstration of joy by the tribe. Major Whitely gave this squaw the name of Susan, which she has borne ever since. A remarkable coincidence in this story is that the rescued Meekers came from Greeley, which is the identical spot where Susan herself was saved from burning by the whites.

The rescue party found the captives picturesquely attired in woollen blanket dresses made by themselves with needles and O. N. T. Miss Josie's costume was the most striking. Her dress was made of an Indian blanket, plain skirt and long jacket waist with tight sleeves. The blanket stuff was dark brown, the broad yellow stripes in the goods acting as a border around the bottom of the dress and the flowing waist. Her feet were encased in moccasins, and on her head was a broad white sombrero. Miss Meeker, though by no means a handsome young lady, is bright and attractive in appearance. She is a blonde and naturally of fair complexion, though now sun-burned. Her hair is cut short to the neck, a sacrifice she made after becoming a captive on account of the vermin which swarmed everywhere.

Mrs. Price is a young lady yet. Though but twenty-three years of age, she has been married eleven years. She is a neutral, naturally bright and active, but just now the death of her husband and her terrible experience has saddened her. Mrs. Price was dressed in a plain woollen dress, which she wore when taken captive. She, however, exchanged it for a "blanket" dress similar to that worn by Miss Meeker. She also wore a *sombrero*. The two little children, May and Johnnie, wore their agency clothes, sadly tattered and torn.

Relating her experience in the camp Miss Meeker says

In camp I worked all the time and so did Mrs. Price. We baked and sewed and kept busy and as cheerful and indifferent as we could. Besides making myself some clothes I made a lot of clothes for the young Indians, at which they were pleased. The Indians said we would be kept there all winter, and so while I expected that such would not be the case, I concluded to make some clothes for myself, especially as those I had were all banged up.

After they were released they stopped all night at Johnson's camp, and started early the next morning on ponies for the wagons, which had been left at the end of the road, about forty miles south toward the Uncompahgre River. General Adams had left them and gone to see the soldiers, so Captain Cline was in charge of the party and the escort to the wagons on the way back. The Indian escort which had accompanied them for a time, left them, and Captain Cline grew suspicious.

He was an old pioneer, had served in the army, and had fought the Indians in New Mexico, and travelled over the western country so much that, although a great friend of Ouray and his Indians, still he was suspicious of these savages, and thought that while the escort had been with the White River Indians they had become corrupted. So when he saw that they had left them he put spurs to his horse and rushed on ahead of the party to where the wagons were. He was afraid that they would cut the harness to pieces or do some mischief to prevent the captives from leaving immediately. This would keep them in the neighbourhood, so that in case General Adams failed in stopping hostilities by a general *powwow* they could recapture them and hold them as hostages for a further treaty.

Captain Cline reached the wagons in a short time and, as he suspected, found the Indians seated around the wagons in a body with most of the blankets lying on the ground already divided among them. They had also got hold of the boxes of provisions and canned fruit which General Adams had brought from Los Pinos for the captives. They had burst them open and were eating the contents. Captain Cline is personally acquainted with many of the Indians, and he completely astonished them. Jumping off his horse he threw the reins on the ground, and, rushing forward in great anger, he shouted: "Chief Ouray shall hear of this, and will settle with you!"

The captain then picked up an axe and began to split kindling wood to prepare for the captives. His object was to keep the axe in his hand and be master of the situation until the main party should arrive. He feared treachery, and, putting on a bold front, he made it pretty lively for the Indians. They fell back, got off the blankets and gave up the canned fruit. Captain Cline threw the blankets on the wagon with what canned provisions there were left. Shortly after this occurrence the party arrived with Major Sherman. They then travelled on to Chief Ouray's house.

Captain Cline was met by Ouray at the gate. The good chief looked at him a moment and said:

"Captain, tell me how you found things when you reached the wagons."

The captain was surprised, but narrated the facts as stated. Ouray listened a moment and, grimly smiling, said:

"Yes, you reached the wagons at such a time and you found Utes around the wagons eating fruit. I know all about it. Ouray not a fool. I had good and true Indians in the mountains around the wagons. They look down and see bad Indians, and then when wagons start safely the good Indians run back to Ouray on fast horses and tell Ouray, and Ouray make up his mind about it. Bad Ute can't fool Ouray."

The chief said this in broken English to the captain, but when he spoke to Mr. Pollock he conversed in eloquent and melodious Spanish, for he had been educated among the Spanish Mexicans of Taos, down on the border, and his words are always delivered with great fluency.

Ralph Meeker, son of the Agent, Inspector Pollock and Dr. J. H. Lacy, the agency physician, came down to meet the ladies within a few minutes after their arrival. Ralph Meeker's meeting with his mother and sister was exceedingly affecting, Mrs. Meeker giving way entirely to her emotion.

They were well treated at Ouray's house. It had Brussels carpet, window curtains, stoves, good beds, glass windows, spittoons, rocking chairs, camp stools, mirrors and an elegantly carved bureau. They were received as old and long-lost friends. Ouray's wife, Chapeta, wept for their hardships, and her motherly face, dusky, but beautiful with sweetness and compassion, was wet with tears. They left her crying.

From this point the party, now headed by Ralph Meeker, took the United States mail coaches, with fleet horses and expert drivers. The journey, over lofty mountains for three days and one night, brought them out of the San Juan country to the swiftly flowing Rio Grande. The Indian reservation was seventy miles behind them. Two ranges of mountains lay between them and that land of captivity and terror. They could not forget the noble Ouray and his true friends who lived there, yet it made their tired hearts beat rapturously when they saw the steam cars at Alamosa.

At Alamosa they remained two days, the guests of Judge C. D. Hayt. Coming on to Denver, they remained two days, and then passed on to Greeley. They were received everywhere most cordially, and were welcomed back in words of love and warmest greeting.

★★★★★★

It may be added that the captives are rapidly recovering from the bad effects of their trying experiences. Mrs. Meeker and Mrs. Price and her babies are at home at Greeley, and Miss Josephine has begun a lecture tour which promises to yield her a rich harvest. She relates her thrilling story in plain, but strong language. Up to this time she has lectured once in Greeley and twice in Leadville. At the latter place she was rapturously received, and after the close of her first lecture the following series of resolutions, offered by Lieutenant Governor Tabor, were adopted by a unanimous and rising vote:

WHEREAS, The citizens of Leadville have assembled this evening to listen to the recital of the foul murder committed on one of the leading citizens of the State at the White River Agency; and

WHEREAS, These Utes occupy the finest and richest portion of Colorado, and utterly refuse to cultivate the soil and allow others to do so,

Resolved, That the whole so-called Ute Reservation is not worth the life of their best friend, whom they so foully massacred on the 29th of September.

Resolved, That we condemn the Indian policy of the United States government, in allowing our citizens to be murdered by the Indian fiends.

Resolved, That the Ute Indians must and shall be removed outside the border of our State, or that it will, be our duty to make them peaceable Indians.

Resolved, That we heartily applaud the resolution and courage of Miss Josephine Meeker in telling the story of the outrages and sufferings endured by herself, her family and associates, and we commend her to the friendship and courtesies of those who desire to know the true inwardness and want of principle of the noble red man.

CHAPTER 13

Biographical Notes

A few words, we are sure, in regard to the careers of those who have figured in this history, will be acceptable to the reader, and render the book all the more complete.

First, as regards Agent Meeker: The annals of Indian crime do not contain mention of a darker deed than the murder of Hon. Nathan C. Meeker—Father Meeker, as he was called throughout Colorado, a name which had taught many who had never seen him to love him. In the death of Father Meeker, a good man has passed away. He was kind and good to all, and to none more than to the Indians. When Mr. Meeker was appointed Agent at White River the Indians were really suffering for want of the food and clothing which the government had failed to furnish them. Some of the preceding agents had utterly neglected their business. The new agent went to work with his accustomed energy, and with that display of conscientiousness which characterized him in all his undertakings and in all of his dealings with his fellow-beings, to make the agency satisfactory both to the government and the Indians. He laboured ever so hard, and pursued an honest, even course.

Mr. Meeker was about sixty-four years old. He was born in Euclid, Ohio, near Cleveland. The place is now known as Callamer. At an early age he began to write poems and stories for the magazines. When he was still in his boyhood he travelled on foot most of the way to New Orleans, where he arrived without money or letters of recommendation. He succeeded in getting work on the local staff of one of the city papers, which barely gave him a living. In a year or two he returned to Cleveland, and taught school until he could earn enough to pay his way to New York, whither he went with the friendship of George D. Prentice, whom he had met during his southern travels.

In New York he was encouraged by N. P. Willis, and he contributed poems and sketches regularly to the New York *Mirror*, a literary journal edited by Willis, and which attracted considerable attention from good writers of that day.

The young man's style was quaint and somewhat melancholy, and his poems were copied, but he could scarcely earn bread to eat and his sufferings were so great that he abandoned poetry for the rest of his life. He managed to raise money enough to enable him to proceed on foot to Pennsylvania, where he taught school and continued his literary studies. Afterward he returned to Ohio, and in 1844, when about thirty years old, married the daughter of Mr. Smith, a retired sea captain, at Claridon, and took his bride to what was known as the Trumbull Phalanx, which was just being organised at Braceville, near Warren, Ohio. The society was a branch of the Brook Farm and the North American Phalanx, of which Hawthorne, Curtis and Greeley were leading members. The Ohio Phalanx was composed of young and ardent admirers of Fourier, the socialist.

There was no free love, but the members lived in a village, dined at common tables, dwelt in separate cottages and worked in the community fields together, and allowed the proceeds of all their earnings to go into a common fund. Manufactories were established, the soil was fertile, and prosperity would have followed had all the members been honest and the climate healthful. Fever and ague ran riot with the weeds, and the most selfish and avaricious of the Arcadian band began to absorb what really belonged to the weaker ones, who did most of the hard labour. Mr. Meeker, who was one of the chief workers, was glad to get away alive with his wife and two boys, the youngest of whom was born shaking with the ague.

Mr. Meeker was the librarian and chief literary authority of the com munity, but he lost most of his books, and when he reached his Cleveland home he had but a few dollars. In company with his brothers he opened a small store and began business on a "worldly" basis; and he prospered so that he was invited to join another com munity, the disciples and followers of Alexander Campbell, a Scotch-Irishman, the founder of the religious sect the members of which, are sometimes called "Campbellites." General Garfield is a follower of this faith, and he became a fellow townsman of Mr. Meeker. The "disciples" were building a large college at Hiram, Ohio, and Mr. Meeker moved his store thither and received the patronage of the school and church.

While there he wrote a book called *The Adventures of Captain Arm-*

strong. In 1856, when the great panic came, he lost nearly everything. Then he moved to southern Illinois, and, with the remnants of his goods, opened a small store near Dongola, in Union county. For several years his boys "ran" the store, while he worked a small farm and devoted his spare hours to literature. His correspondence with the Cleveland *Plaindealer* attracted the attention of Artemus Ward, and the result was a warm and personal friendship. When the war broke out he wrote a letter to the *Tribune* on the south-western political leaders and the resources of the Mississippi Valley. Horace Greeley telegraphed to A. D. Richardson, who was in charge of the *Tribune* at Cairo, this dispatch:

Meeker is the man we want.

Sidney Howard Gay engaged him, and, after serving as a war correspondent at Fort Donelson and other places, at the close of the war Mr. Meeker was called to New York to take charge of the agricultural department and do general editorial work on the *Tribune*. He wrote a book entitled *Life in the West*, and his articles on the Oneida Community were copied into leading German, French and other European journals. In 1869 he was sent to write up the Mormons, but finding the roads beyond Cheyenne blockaded with snow he turned southward and followed the Rocky Mountains down to the foot of Pike's Peak, where he was so charmed with the Garden of the Gods and the unsurpassed scenery of that lovely region, where birds were singing and grasses growing in the mountains, that he said if he could persuade a dozen families to go thither he would take his wife and girls to live and die there. Mr. Greeley was dining at the Delmonico when he heard of it.

"Tell Meeker," exclaimed he, "to go ahead. I will back him with the *Tribune*."

A letter was printed, a meeting held, subscriptions invited, and $96,000 were forwarded to the treasurer immediately. Mr. Meeker was elected president of the colony and Horace Greeley made treasurer. So many applications were sent in that it was thought a larger tract of land would be needed than seemed to be free from encumbrance at Pike's Peak. Several miles square of land were bought on the Cache-la-Poudre River, where the town of Greeley now stands, and several hundred families were established in what had been styled "The Great American Desert." Horace Greeley's one exhortation was:

"Tell Meeker to have no fences nor rum."

On this basis the colony was founded. Today, (at first publication), Greeley has 3,000 population, a hundred miles of irrigating canals, a fine graded school, and it is the capital of a county 160 miles long.

He was one of Colorado's Commissioners to the Centennial Exposition, and soon after Mr. Hayes be came President, Mr. Meeker was appointed agent at White River. Mr. Meeker's plan was to have the Indians raise crops and support themselves in an improved way. He encouraged them to live in log houses, and have some of the miscellaneous conveniences of civilization. It was an experiment and had worked well until the beginning of the past season. A large and effective irrigating canal was built by the Indians, and many acres ploughed by these red farmers. One of the bands favoured this new system, and their chief helped to make peace at the first outbreak. More real agricultural work was accomplished at this agency than at any of the others. The ploughing was done for the benefit of the agency and for the Indians, and not for the agent, as has been reported.

Speaking of appearances at the agency under Mr. Meeker's management, Mr. R. D. Coxe, who visited the place just previous to the outbreak, says:

The agency had been moved since any of the party had been there, and as we came in sight of it, it presented a pretty picture to our eyes. The White River valley at the agency is some half or three-quarters of a mile in width, and is splendidly adapted to agriculture, as well by the ease with which it can be irrigated as by the natural qualities of the soil. Facing the agency buildings, under fence, was a field of fifty acres, in which were growing corn and garden truck, and from which a good crop of wheat had been harvested. Around were the signs of a practical farmer, and under the sheds of the agency were the latest improvements in agricultural implements. Here, thought I, is the model farmer. Another generation will find our dusky neighbours tilling their ranches and pursuing the peaceful avocations of civilization, and the blessing will, rest upon the head of N. C. Meeker. But a herd of horses skirted the fenced field, and it seemed to me they looked with jealous eye upon the growing crops. On the hills upon the other side of the river were large herds of cattle, and everything looked pastoral and quiet.

It needed no introduction to tell us that the tall, angular, grey-headed man who welcomed us to the agency was Father

Meeker. To look at him was to see the ploughs, and harrows and fence wire. He told us to unsaddle at the corral, and after an eight hours' ride over a rough trail, we were not unwilling to do so.

Mr. Meeker went to the White River Agency with his wife and youngest daughter, Josephine, who taught the young Indians and was a general favourite. Mr. William H. Post, of Yonkers, was his "boss farmer" and general assistant. Mr. Post had been a competent and very popular Secretary of the Greeley Colony. He was at the agency at the time of the outbreak.

Mrs. Meeker is sixty-four years old, with black hair, now partly tinged with gray, and blue eyes. She is small in stature, her weight being only ninety pounds. She is the daughter of a sea captain, and was born in Cheshire, Connecticut. She moved with her parents, when a child, to the Western Reserve in Ohio, when the country was a wilderness, and was reared as a pioneer's daughter, with many sisters and brothers. She taught school for several years, and was married at the age of twenty-nine to N. C. Meeker, in Clariden, Geauga county, Ohio. She is the mother of five children.

Miss Josephine Meeker is twenty-two years of age, a blonde, with blue eyes and light hair, and is tall in stature and vivacious in manner and conversation. She was a teacher at the agency and a great favourite among the Indians. She taught the boy of Chief Douglass, and had half a dozen offers of marriage from the Ute braves.

Mrs. Meeker is one of the gentlest and most motherly women, with a heart large enough to embrace all humanity. Her kindly disposition and gentle manner should have protected her from the assault of the veriest brute.

Miss Josie seems to have inherited much of the force and enthusiasm of her father. She appears to have overcome the feeling of disgust, which savages must inspire in any lady, and to have entered on her duty of teaching with the highest missionary spirit.

Around this family were gathered, as help, people peculiarly genial and calculated to win by kindness the regard of the Utes, and whose names have already been published. It may here be stated that the Christian name of Mr. Thompson, which has not yet been given, was Arthur. He was a son of one of the leading citizens of Greeley. The agency was well cared for. Comfortable buildings were erected and fine avenues were laid out. One of these, the main street, which ran as straight as a line from the *cañon* to the agency, was named after Chief Douglass. Mr. Meeker was preparing to plant mountain evergreens on both sides of it. The government Indian farm was enclosed with a neat wire fence, and it produced all kinds of crops. The Indians until the mutiny helped to cultivate the soil. They raised potatoes, beets, turnips, and other vegetables. The white *employés* planted the wheat. In the agency yard Mrs. Meeker had some flowers, such as verbenas, mignonette, petunias and others of a more common sort. The Indians seemed to like the improvements, and they admired the flowers.

On ration days their children were to be seen with bunches of flowers in their hands. A large irrigating canal was built by the Indians under the agent's direction. It afforded water for the whole valley. A good table was set for the *employés*, and they were only charged $3.50 per week, which is much less than is charged at the other agencies, where it is $4.00 and $5.00. The best provisions were used and bought at Rawlins. Mr. Meeker refused to have any Indian blankets or Indian goods in the house, so as to be free from all irregularities or charges of corruption. The Indians frequently ate at his private table, and the chiefs came and went when they pleased. They were treated kindly, but not allowed to take charge of the place, as they sometimes wanted to do.

Among the losses sustained by our troops in the Milk River fight, the most serious was the death of that veteran Indian fighter Major Thomas T. Thornburgh, of the Fourth Infantry. This gallant officer was born in Tennessee, from which State he enlisted as a private in the Sixth Tennessee Regiment of Volunteers in September, 1861. He was in the service from that time until August, 1863. During this term he served for the first five months as a private, for two months as sergeant-major, and for the remainder of his term in the service as lieutenant and adjutant. He took part in the battle of Mill Springs, was with our army when General Morgan made his celebrated retreat from Cumberland Gap to the Ohio River, and participated in the battle of Stone River, September 1st.

He was entered at the United States Military Academy of West Point, and was one of the class of '63 graduates from there June 17, 1867. He was commissioned Second Lieutenant in the Second Artillery, June 17, 1867. After three years' service upon the Pacific and Atlantic coasts, he was regularly promoted, April 21, 1870, and as First Lieutenant of Artillery was appointed Major and Paymaster, April 26, 1875. In this capacity he served upon the staff of Brigadier-General

George Crook, with station at Omaha; but tiring of the inactivity of the life, he sought and effected an exchange with Major G. H. Thomas, Fourth Infantry, May 23, 1878. By this transfer Major Thornburgh stepped above no less than two hundred and fifty captains of infantry and many lieutenants of that corps, whose original commissions antedated his, and procured the command of Fort Fred Steele, in Wyoming Territory.

In the fall of 1878 he was placed in charge of the troops assembled at Sidney, Nebraska, to intercept the Cheyennes. The latter crossed the Union Pacific Railroad near Julesburg, and a few hours later, having been conveyed to this point by a special train, Thornburgh's column was in hot pursuit. The Cheyennes forded the treacherous Platte, with whose shifting quicksands they were familiar, and took refuge for the night in an adjacent *cañon*. Thornburgh followed, but his preparations for an immediate attack were foiled by a dense fog, which rose from the river and enveloped it. In the early morning smouldering fires revealed their late proximity, but the Cheyennes had dispersed. Their trail led fan-shaped into and through the dreaded sand hills. Thornburgh followed, and during the day accomplished not less than eighty miles. For forty-eight hours he wandered through this terrible waste, and was only relieved from extreme hunger and thirst by the timely arrival of Major C. H. Carlton, Third Cavalry, and a battalion of that regiment.

By many his failure was attributed to excess of caution, but perhaps he only avoided then the disaster that has so recently overwhelmed his command. Major Thornburgh was shot in the breast and instantly killed. He was a man of splendid physique, and if not a brilliant soldier, a very earnest, brave, ambitious, and conscientious officer, and a genial, whole-souled gentleman. He was an excellent horseman, and the finest shot in the army. He hunted prairie chicken and grouse with an ordinary Springfield rifle. When Dr. Carver made his superb score with glass balls at Omaha, Major Thornburgh, at the solicitation of his numerous friends, followed and almost equalled it. Immediately subsequent to the fruitless chase after the Cheyennes, a council was held with Red Cloud, Youngman-afraid-of-his-horses, and other prominent Sioux chiefs at Fort Sheridan. At its termination the Indians were in an unusually amiable mood, and facetiously compared the battered carbines in the hands of our cavalrymen to their own handsomely mounted Winchesters.

Major Thornburgh, seizing at random one of the former arms

from a soldier, challenged the group of dusky boasters to a trial of their vaunted weapons. Silver half and quarter dollars thrown into the air, or even nickels, were rarely missed; and the coins being too soon exhausted, they insisted on tempting his unerring aim with potatoes, which, although they grow particularly small in the rugged northwest, he invariably cleft in their flight. The braves stood aghast at such wonderful dexterity, and conferred upon him a euphonious sobriquet in their own language, meaning "The-chief-who-shoots-the-stars."

Major Thornburgh was a brother of the ex-Congressman of that name from Tennessee. He leaves a wife (daughter of Major R. D. Clark, paymaster, and niece of Paymaster-General Alvord, U. S. A.) and two children, a boy and a girl, who are now at Omaha, where his remains were buried with becoming ceremonies.

Lieutenant Weir, who was killed south of White River, was the younger son of Robert W. Weir, a celebrated painter and for many years professor of drawing, etc., at West Point. The latter retired with the pay of Colonel July 25, 1876, being then over sixty-two years of age. The lieutenant's elder brother, an artist, now in Europe, has won a reputation equal to his sire's. Lieutenant Weir was hardly thirty years old. He had a fair face, gray eyes, a light moustache, light brown hair, a pleasant smile, a gentle manner and a cheerful disposition, and he is bewailed by so many of his acquaintances among the troops at Rawlins as to indicate a general grief at his fate. Lieutenant Weir was a native of New York and a graduate of the West Point Military Academy, which he entered as a cadet July 1, 1866. He was appointed a Second Lieutenant in the Fifth Artillery, but was transferred to the Ordnance Department November 1, 1874, receiving a commission of First Lieutenant.

★★★★★★

Of the Indians, the greatest interest centres in Ouray (pronounced U-ra), the head chief or king of the Utes, who has come prominently before the country during the time covered by this history and who was, by no means, unknown before. He is, in many respects—indeed, we may say in all respects—a remarkable Indian; a man of pure instincts, of keen perception, and apparently possesses very proper ideas of justice and right—the friend of the white man and the protector of the Indian, ever standing up and boldly asserting the rights of his tribe, and as continually doing all in his power to create favour for the white man with the Indians.

Ouray, in telling the story of his life, says that he was born in Taos

Valley, N. M., near the Pueblo village of that name, in 1839, His tribe of Utes were in the habit of spending much of their time in the Taos Valley, and San Luis Park, and along the Sangre de Cristo Mountains. Down in this region they were accustomed to meet the Apaches, who came up from the north. It is a very common thing for the women of a tribe of Indians to marry out of their tribe. Ouray's father married an Apache woman; hence the epithet which is so often sneeringly applied to Ouray by those of the Indians who dislike him, of being an "Apache *papoose*." The Indians became so accustomed to associating with the Mexicans that some of them began to adopt the customs of this people, and when Ouray's father and mother came to the conclusion that they wanted to be married, they quietly marched up to the little adobe church which stands on the hill, in the village at Red River crossing, and had the priest perform the ceremony, just as any good Catholics would. And when Ouray was born, they took him to the same *adobe* building and had him baptised into the Catholic Church—the only instance on record of the kind.

Ouray had three brothers and two sisters, but he survives all of his brothers, while both of his sisters still live, one of them near the home of the chief on the Uncompahgre and the other is Susan, the wife of Chief Johnson, of the White River Tribe, who so signally distinguished herself in her kindness to the Meeker women and Mrs. Price while they were captives among the tribe.

Ouray has long been a chief among the Utes, but is more renowned for his wisdom than his bravery. During his young manhood, however, he was accustomed to lead the Ute braves to battle and was a very brave as well as successful fighter. He generally planned well and fought bravely. During these times the Utes were engaged in a deadly encounter with the Arapahoes, Cheyennes and Sioux. It was a war between the plains Indians and the mountain tribes, between Highlanders and Lowlanders. Ouray entered into the spirit which characterized his race with a will, and soon became a renowned warrior. He soon was famed for wisdom, and his counsel was sought by the Utes far and near. When the white men first began to settle what is now Colorado, they found Ouray chief of the Tabequache or Uncompahgre tribe, the largest band of the tribe and in great favour with the members of other bands, so that while he was not head chief, he was a man of the greatest influence and power among his people.

He was also disposed to be friendly towards the white settlers and soon be came known as a mediator between the two races. He con-

HEAD CHIEF OF THE UTES

tinued increasing his authority and influence among his people until, as he expresses it, "the year after Lincoln's death," he was recognised as head chief by the Indians. In 1873 he acted as interpreter between the Indians and Commissioner Brunot, in the conference looking to the cession to the government of the San Juan country, and in recognition of his services at that time and in the past, the government settled an annuity of $1,000 upon him, which he has since continued to draw regularly. He made his first trip to Washington during the same year that he was made head chief.

The Utes have had five wars with the Arapahoes, and Ouray states that during some of these he led as many as seven hundred warriors to the battlefield. The second war occurred about 1858, and some of the battles were fought just above where Denver stands. Ouray had but thirty men with him, while the Arapahoes numbered seven hundred. They came upon the Utes in the morning, just before daylight, and took the mountain Indians completely by surprise. However, Ouray rallied his few warriors, and they hurriedly formed in a square, after retreating a short distance, and after a fight which continued fourteen hours, repulsed the Arapahoes.

It was during this fight that Ouray lost his little boy—the only son that has been born to him. He says that when he saw the Arapahoes coming, he threw water in the face of the child, then six years of age, for the purpose of awaking him, but failing in this, he threw covering over him and left him to go and fight the invaders of the camp. But the entire day passed before he could extricate himself from the entanglements involving him, and when he did get away and have an opportunity to return to his *tepee*, his boy had disappeared and has never since been seen by his father. This incident is still vividly remembered by Ouray, and he never refers to it without manifesting the greatest sorrow over it. He professes to believe his boy is dead, though he knows he is not. He is still with the Arapahoes, and as Ouray heartily despises the Arapahoes, he would prefer the death of his son to the disgrace implied in being an Arapahoe. This feeling on his part most likely explains the representation of the matter as made by the old chief.

Ouray has never been able to get his boy back, though he has made every effort to recover him. The government, too, has done all in its power to restore Ouray's son to him. Mr. Brunot himself made a strong effort. But the boy declines to go back, or to be talked to upon the subject. It seems that he has imbibed Arapahoe ideas, and that he utterly despises the Utes. This is really what most hurts old Ouray. His family pride is injured. He thinks his son has been utterly disgraced. The boy is a good-looking Indian. He is now about thirty years old. He has been adopted by Chief Friday, and, it is said, stands a good show of becoming chief, whenever that renowned warrior shall "*cross the range.*"

Ouray has lived at his present home on the Uncompahgre and in that vicinity during the past twenty-three years, having resided, previous to establishing himself at that point, in New Mexico. Chopeta, his present wife, is his second, his first having been the mother of his boy and also of a girl child, now dead. Ouray lives in good style. He owns a farm, which is a real garden spot, of three hundred acres. Of this he cultivates about a hundred acres, raising all kinds of cereals and vegetables. He lives in a neatly built and commodious *adobe* house built for him by the government and neatly furnished and carpeted. He owns great numbers of horses and a good many cattle and sheep, and. when he goes out rides in a carriage which was a present from ex-Governor McCook. He hires labourers from among the Mexicans and Indians, and also expects his wife to do her share of the farm work.

Ouray's present wife, Chopeta, is kind-hearted and very much like Ouray in her nature, being kind and well disposed towards the whites. The chief has become very much attached to his present manner of living, and it is said is disposed to remain on his farm and surrender the reins of government to some younger man. Speaking before the commission, of which he is a member, now investigating the present trouble, at Los Pinos, on the 16th of November of the present year he said:

> I do not want to be a chief. I grow old and am tottering. Let some young man with the fire of youth in his veins take my place. I have my farm, which I would rather cultivate and watch the seed planted by me grow up to maturity than to be head chief. They all come to me with their troubles. I know everything and have all their burdens to bear. Washington no want me to give up my position, wants me to stay and govern Utes. I want only to be.known as Ouray, the friend of the white man.

So far as the present difficulty is concerned, Ouray has continued from first to last friendly to the whites and an advocate of peace. As soon as he learned of the Thornburgh fight he sent runners to White River ordering that hostilities cease. He also did every thing in his power to secure the surrender of the captive women, and when there was a prospect of the southern Utes breaking out, he sent timely warning to the white settlers near. He has pursued a straight forward and manly course and deserved the honour which the government conferred upon him in making him a member of the commission.

Although baptised into the Catholic Church, Ouray does not professes the white man's religion. Senoughlbase is the Ute god, and in him Ouray believes. He says that when good people die they will go to a delightful place like a beautiful valley, with a clear stream of water running in it, there to meet with the friends and the spirits of friends who have gone before. They will all meet there—friends, brothers and parents. He speaks with much tenderness of his father and mother. He also believes there is a bad place where bad people cannot meet their friends who have preceded them.

One little instance may be related as going to show the character of Ouray and the manner of his dealing with his inferiors. Since he became head chief he has promoted Sapavanaro, Shavano, Waro and Billy to chieftainships under himself among the Uncompahgre Utes. He has made Ignacio head chief of the Southern Utes, and Pavisatch second chief of the Southern Utes. As is often the case with people making greater pretensions to civilization, most of these fellows scorn the hand that feeds them. Ignacio has grown unfriendly to Ouray, and Waro and Billy seem to have deserted him for the White River Utes.

Cojoe, who has figured extensively in this narrative already, was in favour at Ouray's court at one time, being the chief medicine man of the Tabequache tribe. He, and not Ouray, as has frequently been asserted, was the man who killed the young brave Osepah, during the summer of 1878. Osepahwasan ambitious young man, and was working hard to secure the coveted prize, a chieftainship. He saw that a number of the tribe were displeased with the farming operations of Ouray, and his notorious friendship to the whites, and thought that by making himself the mouthpiece of the tribe, he would acquire great renown and their admiration. Consequently, he rode to Ouray's house, meeting the chief on his way to the agency. Cojoe had just come in from a hunt, and with his rifle slung on his shoulder, was accompanying Ouray.

Osepah stopped them, and dismounting from his horse, laid before Ouray the fact that he was wanted no longer as their chief; that he was a white man at heart, and ought to join the whites, concluding with a perfect tirade of abuse, in which he called the chief "a squaw," the most degrading epithet that can be applied to an Indian, and one which he is generally quickest to resent. Ouray took no notice of the speech, regarding it as the insane utterances of a hot headed young man; but not so Cojoe. Waiting until Osepah had mounted his horse and ridden several rods away, he unslung his rifle, took deliberate aim, and Osepah fell dead with a bullet through his brain. For this offense Cojoe was expelled by Ouray from the tribe and went to White River, most probably being concerned in the murder of the employés there. He now is arrayed in a dress-coat, with two gold chains dangling from his pocket. Ouray says that he will never again return to the agency, his conduct having given him more trouble than that of all the rest of his Indians.

Captain Billy has generally professed friendship for the whites, though he has been a great deal among the White River Utes since the troubles of which we write began. He paid a visit to Washington in the fall of 1878. Bill is a brother of Jack, though much more kindly disposed. He really looks like an in offensive Indian, but he has plenty of Indian fire in his brain. At one time he boasted that no lead could kill him, and when one of the tribe said he would like to try, Bill stood up, folded his arms, and said, "Fire" The bullet went through his left side below the ribs. Bill laughed, and said, "I told you lead no kill me." He was laid up about two weeks, and came out all right.

During the present disturbance Douglass and Jack, both White River chiefs, have attracted more attention than any other two Indians. They are quite intelligent fellows, though very different in appearance, stature, physique, temperament and manner. Douglass is rather short—about five feet six or seven inches in heigh— of medium build, about fifty years of age, and with a decidedly German cast of countenance. His complexion is rather darker than most of his tribe. Mr. A. D. Coxe, formerly of Middle Park, now residing in Quincy, Ill., who visited White River Agency, describes Douglass as follows:

As we approached the corral a figure came toward us from the direction of the river, that I gazed at with increasing interest as it approached. Dressed in what I should call the fall attire of a workman in the States, I set myself to solve the problem of what nationality. White, red or black? Once it was a sunburned white man, then a "nigger," but when it reached us the inevitable red smear betrayed it. It was an Indian, and, moreover, an Indian who spoke respectable English. There was something I should describe as a reserved force in his manner (not matter) of speaking. Our conversation was trivial. I had put my estimate on him, and it was that he had grown civilized enough to doff the blanket (emblem of the aborigine) and to become generally no account. Imagine my surprise when the sheriff turned to me and told me our visitor was Douglass. I had expected to find the great chief in a mud palace, exacting the reverence and homage of all comers. In stead, he is an Indian who would be taken for a respectable negro church sexton in Kentucky, and he keeps up the likeness by his grave reticence and respectful curiosity as to what our mission is. Douglass is about five feet seven inches in height, medium stature and outrageously bow-legged. The most noticeable thing about him is that he shaves, but manages to escape an iron-gray growth of moustache on the sides of his mouth in that operation. In his dress he made no pretence to the gaudy—was satisfied with the substantial.

Douglass was made a chief among the White River Utes in 1869, and been considered a friend of the whites. He has ever professed the warmest regard for his pale face brothers, and when Agent Meeker first went to White River was among the first to manifest a friendly feeling towards the old gentleman. He sent his boy to school when Miss Josephine established her institution for teaching the young Indian how not to shoot, and seemed in every way satisfied with his lot and surroundings. But it now appears that he has all this time been merely simulating friendship, and that all the while he has harboured a deep-rooted feeling against the Americans. His treatment of Mrs. Meeker and her daughter, the part he took in the massacre and his confessions to Mrs. Price are proof positive of his bad feeling. It has also been recently charged that he took a prominent part in the Mountain Meadow massacre. The Indians themselves assert that he did, but Douglass when questioned concerning this accusation replied:

"No; me no fight. Me no chief then; papers heap lies."

Even to the most unobservant, he displayed great agitation, which, in an Indian, is extremely uncommon, while speaking, and it would not be at all surprising, if the facts can be obtained, that this maltreater of helpless women and coward as well, should prove to have been concerned in this massacre. Mrs. Price's characterization of him as "the smartest and meanest of the Utes" may be classified as accurate.

Ouray being asked about Douglass could not be brought to tell much of the history of this chief, saying that Douglass was not a very brave man, but great in the council. His speeches are always eloquent, generally to the point, and always convincing. Through his tongue, he has acquired about the same influence over his band that Jack has through his bravery, and when a question is hanging in suspense in one of the Ute councils, that voice turns the balance. He speaks English very imperfectly, but appears to be good natured, though decidedly taciturn and thoughtful. Even to his own people he says little, and what he says is in a low tone and in short paragraphs. He impresses one as having considerable ability, though not as being as intelligent as Jack. This, however, may be due to the different manner of his Lieutenant, and the fact that the latter has travelled as far east as Boston, while Douglass has never crossed the Missouri.

Jack is far more the typical Indian than his leader. Some five feet ten or eleven inches in height, straight and slender, but strong and sinewy. He has a narrow forehead, prominent, hooked nose, protruding cheek bones, large, black eyes and an immense mouth. His complexion is that of a bright *mulatto*. His straight black hair falls is profusion over his shoulders and he wears large hoop earrings and a silver medal about three inches in diameter, which was presented to him by the government and of which he is very proud. One edge of it is deeply indented, he says, by a bullet fired at him by Piah. His eyes flash when he speaks of this little experience, and he suggests a purpose of returning the compliment whenever a suitable opportunity shall offer.

Another article which he particularly prizes is a pipe of polished red stone, which he says was captured from the Sioux. He carries it in an ornamented buckskin case and cleans it with the utmost tenderness every time it is smoked. He usually dresses in a complete suit of buckskin, but wears a black slouch hat. He is something of a dandy and had a good deal of ornamental work on his clothing as well as on his pipe and gun cases embroidered with coloured porcupine quills and beads. He is generally armed, even in time of peace, with a first-rate Winchester rifle and his belt is full of cartridges. His pose and manner are dignified and graceful, and he is exceedingly jovial in disposition; though a serious, thoughtful look comes into his eyes when he is at business. He knows more of the world than his fellows, and consequently respects and fears the whites more. He talks English quite well and likes to talk.

Ouray says:

Jack was always a brave man. When he was a boy he was taken by a white family to Salt Lake City, as a sort of page, and was petted greatly by them. He resided there about a year, and probably learned what English he knows at that time. Being taken to task by his mistress one day about some trivial offence, Jack then threw a knife at her, cutting her severely in the head, and started for Colorado. He has had two duels with members of his own tribe, and in each came off victorious, in the last one, after disabling his opponent by a stab, lassoing him and dragging him at his horse's tail until nothing was left save a mangled mass of flesh. The Utes all know of Jack's bravery, and know his great influence over his band. "Said Ouray, "Jack will fight three white men; but he no hide and shoot them when they come past. When Jack say to white man, 'You my friend,' all right. When he say, 'You no stay here,' white man better go.

Previous to this present outbreak Jack was considered friendly to the whites. He was about Denver a great deal, and received considerable attention from the people here. But he objected strongly to the innovations which Father Meeker attempted to introduce, and when it came time to take up arms he headed the hostiles. Previous to this he said it was useless for the Indians to fight the white man, for they would certainly get the worst of it in the end. And he fully appreciated what he said. He had witnessed the great extent and power of our people, and seemingly profited by what he saw. He went so far as to invite the whites to settle on the reservation saying that they and the Indians should be great friends.

Johnson gained his chieftainship by a daring act of valour in the last war of the Utes with the Arapahoes. One day their scouts having reported none of the enemy near, Johnson, then a stripling, and two companions started out on a hunt. They had gone about twenty miles from their camp when they were at tacked by eight Arapahoes. Johnson's two friends were killed, and he only escaped by leaving his horse and concealing himself in a river or stream flowing near. The Arapahoes took all three horses and started for their camp, Johnson following them on foot. When they camped for the night Johnson crept up, stabbed the sentinel and the other seven, took their scalps and horses, and returned to his friends to tell the story. For this instance of prowess he received the chieftainship of the band which he now commands.

Although a brave Indian, Johnson differs from Jack in that he will, if he can, take an unfair advantage of an enemy, and should he bear one a grudge, will not hesitate to ambuscade and shoot him. His wife, Ouray's sister, was given to him as a further recognition of his services against the Arapahoes. Johnson is also the best shot among the Utes, with both the bow and rifle, and his *tepee*, after a hunt, contains more game than any of the rest. Johnson has recently acted as chief medicine man at White River, and he figures in Mr. Meeker's letters as Dr. Johnson. He is about forty-five.

The next most noted of the hostile chiefs is Colorado, pronounced and generally spelled Colorow. He is a bully and a coward, and commands the loathing and the disrespect of both white man and Indian. He is a renegade among the White River Utes, and at one time had attained considerable influence among this band, rising to the chieftainship of a quite respectable number. But he was deposed from power, for which result ex-Governor McCook is highly responsible. Formerly, the State government was made in some way responsible for the care of the Indians. During McCook's administration, Colorow and a band of Utes came to this city and camped on the out skirts. One day the chief sent word that he wanted a new tent. McCook dispatched an agent to see in what condition Colorow's tent was, and the report was that he did not need a new tent, and McCook accordingly refused him. In the afternoon, while the governor was in his office, Colorow came in half drunk, with a revolver in his hand, and came over where McCook was writing and sat down. The governor took in the situation at a glance, but did not look up.

"McCook, liar!" said Colorow.

The governor went on writing.

"McCook, dam liar!" said the chief.

Still McCook continued. with his work.

"McCook, heap d—m liar!" said Colorow, reaching a climax.

Nevertheless, McCook would not look at him.

By this time Colorow had concluded that there was no fight in the governor and allowed the hand containing the revolver to drop to his side. The move was a fatal one. In an instant McCook seized his wrist, knocked the weapon away from him, and, catching the astonished Indian by the neck, kicked him downstairs and out into the street, where there were a number of Utes standing about. With great tact McCook pointed to the prostrate and humiliated form of Colorow, and turning to the Utes, said: "No man to lead braves. Colorow old woman. Get

143

COLOROW

a man for a chief." Then turning on his heel, he walked upstairs. The next day the mortified Utes deposed Colorow.

Colorow still, however, boasts a considerable following among the worst of the Utes, if such a distinction is allowable. He is old and chubby, and presents the worst appearance of all the tribe.

Piah is the chief of the Middle Park Utes. He is a clever fellow enough, but very deceitful. He has been to Washington, New York and Boston, as have some of the others. Piah says he got shaved in Washington, which accounts for the few hairs on his chin, of which he is very proud. In conversation with him, he said, "Washington heap big, heap big houses; New York heap big, big houses, big boats; plenty white men;" and so of other Eastern cities; but at the end he says, "White man heap no good, heap lie. Indian no lie." Upon being asked what the great white father said to him, his answer was:

> White father at Washington said Indian must make potato, cab-bage, and work. I tell white father no make potato, cabbage, no work; Indian hunt, fish. No hunt, no fish, Indian fight and die. Me great warrior. Warriors no plough. Me go to Washington and see John Grant. (The Indians all call Grant "John.") John Grant great warrior. He no work. Me see John Grant's squaw. She no work, either, too. Great warriors no work. Tell you what do. You say to John Grant he come here and go with me. We go out and fight 'Rapahoes and Cheyennes, and kill plenty braves, and get plenty squaws. Then squaws work and me and John Grant have bully good time. No work; no plough; no nothing.

Washington is another chief supposed to have been engaged in the recent fighting—at any rate, in the depredations committed along the frontier. He is getting to be an old Indian, and is remarkable for the extreme low cunning of his countenance and his stove pipe hat, which has long ago seen its best days.

Describing the appearance of this chief, Mr. Coxe, whom we have above quoted, says:

> I think that Washington is about as ugly a biped as we have at present on the continent, and what homeliness of face he lacked, he had attempted to supply by dress. I am not a good hand at description of dress, but I shall endeavour to tell you how Washington was attired. His head was surmounted by a soft hat, turn-down rim, which was ornamented by a band of calico. He had on a red flannel shirt, soiled and torn, and about

as poor a pair of pantaloons as the law allows. But the leggings, the one article of the dress of equestrians which the Indians make better than the whites, were handsome. An old and ragged pair of boots protected his feet. As he came up I saw he was cross-eyed, and that the 'whites' of his eyes had become 'browns,' as well as bloodshot.

There are, of course, many other chiefs among the tribes, but those which we have described are the most noted, and most of them have taken prominent part in the late outbreak.

Conclusion

It remains to be stated that at the present writing, November 25, 1879, there is a commission in the field, appointed by the Secretary of the Interior, the Hon. Carl Schurz, to investigate the recent troubles with a view to bringing the guilty to justice and arriving at some means of settling the Indian difficulties in Colorado. This commission consists of General Edward Hatch, of the army; General Charles Adams, special agent of the post-office department, and Chief Ouray. The meetings of the commission are held in a log hut, built for a stable, at Los Pinos, or Uncompahgre Agency. Ouray early sent a message to the hostile Indians, ordering them to meet the commission at his agency.

All the leaders except Jack came to the agency. Douglass, Johnson, and Sewerwick were examined, and all appeared before the commission with sullen countenances, "armed to the teeth," and all declared unequivocally that they knew nothing. At one time the commission seemed in imminent danger of losing their lives. Even Ouray veered about, put on his Indian clothes, and appeared thoughtful and ferocious. General Hatch had previously sent for a detachment of soldiers as an escort, who appeared, most likely, in time to be of good service in frightening the Indians and preventing ill treatment of the commission.

Ouray has made a proposition to have a delegation of the hostiles sent to Washington to treat with the secretary, but the secretary has virtually declined to grant them this privilege, whereat the Indians are matter stands. The hostiles have gone back to their mountain retreats and probably expect to remain there during the winter. It is probably not well to make predictions in a book which may so soon as is the prospect in this case be verified or prove unfounded, but we feel perfectly safe in saying that if the Indians are to be punished for their past offences the army will yet be compelled to take the matter in hand, either this winter or during the coming spring.

★★★★★★

We have refrained in our narrative from burdening it with opinions of our own concerning the events which we have related, believing that the facts speak for themselves and that the more boldly they are allowed to stand forth in their own natural ugliness, the more apt they will be to impress upon the reader the true condition of Indian affairs in Colorado. Our position is not a halfway one. We join in the chorus that comes up from the entire State, from the entire west, alike from the plains and from the mountains, and the gist of which is that the Indians must go. In this State we confine ourselves to the Utes. They have been a hindrance and a drawback to Colorado's progress, occupying a third of the area of the State. Standing in the way of the march of civilization, for bidding schools, preventing settlement, keeping out railroads, they are a pest and a nuisance. More than this, they are murderers and thieves—criminals of the worst character, malicious towards the whites and bent upon doing all they can to annoy and injure the race.

So far as their rights are concerned, they have, if they ever had any, forfeited them by their own conduct. They have robbed the white people, burned the forests, destroyed the game and murdered a hundred men. They are savages because they will not become civilized. They lie and steal and murder because they prefer doing so to adopting the customs and manners of the white people, and not because they do not know that it is wrong and against the law of the land to do these things. The people of the west will never be satisfied until the murderers of Thornburgh and his soldiers and of Agent Meeker and the agency *employés*, atone for these deeds with their own blood. The death of one or two or a dozen will not be sufficient to satisfy justice, but all who took part in the bloody work must be punished. And the other Utes should be accommodated at some other place. It will be better for them and better for the whites. The opinion prevails throughout the State that the land now occupied by the Indians is rich in mineral. There are ten thousand prospectors along the border, casting wistful eyes to the land beyond which they believe to abound in mineral treasure. Many have ventured over and have found what they sought.

All who have crossed the line have determined to return, and their reports have decided many others to follow them. It may safely be predicted that three thousand prospectors will invade the Ute reserva-

148

tion land next spring. These men can not understand why gold and silver should exist right under their noses, though it be on an Indian reservation, lying there like capital buried, and they not be allowed to dig it out and put it to use. We agree with them. The mineral is there, and the miners and prospectors, upright to a man, who are courageous and hardy enough to undertake to get it, should have it. Frontier life in the mountains is hard enough and perilous enough at best. Bad roads, the distance from home and the necessities of life, and hard climate, are sufficient of themselves, without adding danger from Indians.

These frontiersmen, whether in Massachusetts or Virginia, Ohio or Kentucky, Wisconsin or Missouri, Colorado or the Black Hills, in whatever part of the continent they may go, have opened up the way for the advance of the white man and civilization. To them the present prosperity and extent of the country are due. To them the existence of North America is wholly due—not to any presuming Secretary of the Interior or Boston Tract Society. These noble men should be protected in their work. Though, of course, self-interest is with most of them the impelling motive, they nevertheless do mankind a vast service in their advances into the new and wild lands, opening up new sources of wealth and new places for homes. But the prospectors expect to explore the western border of Colorado next year, whether it be pleasant to a half-dozen men at Washington, who know really nothing about the matter which they control, or attempt to control, or not; or whether the Indians are there or not. If the Indians are not removed, conflicts are inevitable, and many valuable lives, not only those of prospectors but those of families in settlements off the reservation, are sure to be sacrificed.

What Colorado asks is:
That the Utes who took part in or inspired the Thornburgh fight and the agency massacre, be executed.
That the remaining members of the tribe be re moved to some reservation outside the bounds of the State.

What the West asks is:
That the Indians of all tribes and nations be gathered at one place, Indian Territory for example.
That they be made to earn their own living as other men and women are, or allowed to starve.
That the control of them be left to the army as a police force to preserve and compel order, and not to contrive devices to *induce* the

Indians to be good—to coerce them into proper habits.

The following resolutions, adopted by a mass meeting of the people of Greeley, the town founded and guided to prosperity by Mr. Meeker, we consider a fit conclusion of this volume of frontier history:

Resolved, That while paying tribute to our deceased friends and neighbours, we would gladly cherish a hope that this awful sacrifice may somehow serve to lessen the volume of atrocity incident to our Indian policy.

Resolved, That the government be called upon through our representatives in Congress to make full compensation for all private property destroyed by this outbreak, and to suitably pension all persons who were dependent for support upon our friends and neighbours who were killed.

Resolved, That we heartily commend the prompt and diligent efforts of Governor Pitkin to protect the citizens of the State from Indian ravages ever since the hostile attitude of the Utes became apparent.

Resolved, That we mournfully deprecate the great apparent neglect of Mr. Meeker's touching appeal for relief made as early as the 10th of September last.

Resolved, That we indignantly denounce the grace less insinuations and gratuitous assertion of some eastern papers that this defection among the Utes is the result of bad faith on the part of the agent and people of Colorado, as wholly unfounded in fact, and made in a fault-finding spirit among people entirely ignorant of the situation, and of the Indian character.

Resolved, That the idea so often offered by Congress that the Indian is the ward of the government, merits the application of a policy more analogous to the humane principles of the common law of "Guardian and ward" than any hitherto adopted by the government.

Resolved, That, conceding the embarrassment incident to the proper solution of the Indian question, we insist that the constant breeding of a horde of savages in the central part of the continent, maintaining them in idleness as wards of the government, without restricting influences, providing them with the best weapons of destruction, appears, after so many years of experience, like a special invention of evil genius to make savage warfare and atrocities inevitable and frequent.

Resolved, That so long as the most romantic portions of our domain are to be especially dedicated as nurseries of barbarism, we insist that, so fast as the Indian is thus bred up, equipped and fitted for his treacherous warfare, and found hostile and determined to kill and murder; he be certainly slain, and no more fed and petted as a ward.

Resolved, That all efforts to civilize the Indians must prove futile as long as they are permitted to retain their tribal relations, indulge in barbarous practices, taught to regard themselves as independent nationalities, to be treated with, upon an equal footing, like a foreign country, and as such, pampered with the idea of a sovereign right to make war against the government for any fancied grievance.

Resolved, That the first requirement in the process of civilizing the Indian, is to teach him a sense of responsibility to the government, which supports and protects him; whereas, under the policy which has so long obtained, he derives no such lesson, but, on the contrary, is habitually impressed with the idea that the government owes him a living, and has no right to his loyalty or obedience in return, he should either be accorded the same rights as a citizen, or should be regarded as irresponsible and dangerous, and rigidly kept in restraint.

Resolved, That while the Indian is allowed to remain within the limits of a State, he should be subject to the police regulations of the State and governed and punished by its law and authority. Finally, be it

Resolved, As the sense of this people, that the Indians within the limits of our State are a hindrance to its proper development, and a constant menace to the safety of the people; that by their recent unprovoked and inexcusable depredations they have forfeited all claims to remain among us; and we insist as our ultimatum in this matter that the death penalty be inflicted upon the fiendish murderers of our friends; and that the Utes be speedily removed beyond the borders of Colorado.

Two hundred thousand people pray for this result.

Besieged by the Utes: The Massacre of 1879

On the defensive—the cartridge bag

Contents

The Massacre of 1879

In the summer of 1879 trouble occurred between the White River Utes and their agent, N. C. Meeker. The cause is not important, but the trouble finally became serious enough to warrant the call upon the Secretary of War for the support of troops to repress turbulence and disorder amongst the Indians of that nation. In September an expedition was organized in the department of the Platte, and the following troops were ordered out: one company of the 4th Infantry under Lieutenant Butler D. Price; Troop E, 3rd Cavalry, Captain Lawson commanding; and two troops, D. (Lt. J. V. S. Paddock) and F (Captain J. S. Payne), of the 5th Cavalry. Major T. T. Thornburgh, 4th Infantry, commanded the whole, and Acting Assistant-Surgeon Grimes was the medical officer.

This command was concentrated at Fort Steele, Wyoming, on the Union Pacific Railroad, and marched south from that point towards White River Agency about the 21st of September. Nothing of an unusual character occurred during the first few days of the march, nor was it supposed that anything of a serious nature would happen. The agent had asked for one hundred soldiers and more than double that number were in this column. The troops were *en route* to a certain point to preserve order, not expecting to make war. The Utes understood that, and the very evening preceding their attack upon the troops, the chiefs entered the soldiers' camp, partook of their hospitality, and assured them of their friendship. The report of General Crook says:

> The last message Meeker ever sent to Thornburgh was to the effect that the Indians were friendly and were flying the United States flag. Yet, in the face of all this, the very next morning these Indians, without provocation, treacherously lay in ambuscade and attacked the troops with the result already known.

This, General Crook says, is not war, it is murder; and the general, as usual, is correct. But is it not strange that, with all the horrible examples furnished us in past years, we have never been in the habit of preparing for murder as well as war? It seems at least unfortunate that all our Indian wars must of necessity be inaugurated with the massacre or defeat of the first detachment. It may be interesting, if not instructive, to give a few examples.

The Modoc War of 1872, in which so many valuable lives were lost, was begun by the advance of half a troop of the 1st Cavalry. This force rode up to the Indian camp, dismounted, and were standing to horse, with probably no thought of being murdered or of any serious trouble. It is reported that while the officer in command was talking to the chief a rifle was discharged by an Indian, either accidentally or as a signal, and that instantly thereafter firing on the troops took place and a number were killed and wounded. The Indians, about sixty in number, taking advantage of the confusion among the troops, retired to their stronghold in the lava beds, murdering every white man *en route*. In this stronghold they defied the government, massacred a commission composed of prominent men sent to them in peace, and withstood the attacks of 1300 soldiers for months, and until both food and water gave out.

The Nez Percé's War in 1877 commenced in about the same way. Two small troops of cavalry, marching down a deep and long canon, presented themselves before the camp of Chief Joseph, as if a display of this nature was all that was necessary to capture a force of two hundred and fifty warriors. The Indian, always quick to see an advantage and to profit by it, was not slow in this instance, and the first few shots from the enemy on the left and rear of the line caused a hasty retreat of the soldiers, who no doubt up to that time thought there was to be *nothing serious*.

The Little Big Horn fight in 1876, where General Custer and most of his command were massacred, was surely the result of overestimating one's strength and underrating that of the enemy.

Other examples could be furnished, but are not these, with their attendant losses and failures, sufficient to prove that with the Indian as a foe we must always be prepared, and especially careful when he seems most friendly and still holds on to his rifle? On the other hand, many instances are known where troops have met and overcome at the start more serious obstacles than those mentioned above, and without a shot being fired. A column on the march, prepared to fight

On outpost duty

if necessary, is not likely to be disturbed, and it is almost certain that no Indians will be seen or heard from unless they have all the advantages, and unless certainty of success follows their first efforts.

This Ute campaign was a repetition of all the other sad occurrences in Indian warfare. Major Thornburgh, the commander, as noble and brave a man as ever marched with troops, fell as others had, having ignored an enemy in the morning who had the power to defeat him before noon. The march through these mountains and into the valley of Milk River, as described, was made as any march would be conducted on a turnpike through a civilized country and among friends. No danger had threatened; on the contrary, the Indians appeared friendly, and assuring messages had been received from the agent.

Thornburgh, not having had experience with Indians and trusting to appearances, anticipated no trouble, and consequently was wholly unprepared when the attack was made. We can in a measure account for such action on the part of a commander when it is remembered that with some men the desire to appear before their troops free from undue anxiety is greater than their sense of caution. Considering the number of troops in this command, and the fact that not half that number of Indians were opposed to them, it is fair to presume that with proper precaution the command might have gone through to the agency without losing a life, or even hearing a shot; but the officers and men following Thornburgh doubtless like him had no thought of danger to such a column; and had the colonel made sufficient preparation to secure his command, and reached his destination safely on that account, he would have been pronounced an "old granny" for having unduly harassed his troops when no enemy appeared.

The employment of the chiefs, ostensibly as guides, but really detaining them as hostages, would have insured the peace as well as the safety of the command beyond a doubt.

But to go more into details: Thornburgh, after leaving his infantry company at a supply camp, pushed on with his three troops of cavalry, and while on the march on the 29th of September, at 10 a. m., at the crossing of Milk River, the Indians opened fire on the column from all directions, and from what followed it would appear that the command was completely surprised, or sufficiently so to make some confusion among the troops. F Troop, 5th Cavalry, and E Troop, 3rd Cavalry, were quickly brought into line, and for some time fought well and bravely, but the superior tactics of the Indian, in his usual role of turning the flanks, and the loss of many brave men including the commander,

BEHIND THE BREASTWORK

soon caused a retreat, and these two troops fell back perhaps half a mile to a point where Lieutenant Paddock, in command of D Troop, 5th Cavalry, and the wagon train, had corralled his train, formed his troop, and was prepared to receive and shelter his comrades.

It is not known what orders Lieutenant Paddock had from his commanding officer as to his duties with the rearguard and wagon train, but it is supposed that as no precautions were being taken in front, none were ordered in rear, so that the prompt action of this young officer in arranging his wagon train and troops for a stand, and holding every man to his duty there, was praiseworthy, and was the means of saving many lives. This afforded shelter and a rallying place for the scattered troopers, then being outflanked and driven back by the enemy; indeed, Paddock's command was even receiving attention from the Indians in the way of rifle-balls, for the Indians knew if they could get the train, they could capture or kill the rest of the command before it could escape from the valley.

Here there was a halting place, and the whole command was concentrated behind and about the wagons. The Indians then surrounded the soldiers, fired upon them from all directions, and, setting fire to the grass, advanced to within a short distance of the wagons, being screened by the thick smoke from the fire of the troops. In this situation the battle was carried on for the rest of that day, the troops being strictly on the defensive, and keeping behind the wagons, while the Indians, lying close to the ground and concealed as much as possible, were able to kill most of the animals and occasionally to pick off a soldier or teamster.

The loss of the animals and the number of wounded men to be cared for and protected made any movement from this spot out of the question. There was nothing to do then but fight it out and hold on until reinforcements could reach them. However, the longest day must have an end, and the sun aided these harassed soldiers by disappearing behind the hills and affording them, under cover of darkness, an opportunity to prepare for the morrow. This first night was employed by the troops in building a breastwork near the water, and in caring for the wounded.

There being no timber within reach, shelter had to be constructed from such material as was at hand. The wagons were unloaded and spare parts used, bundles of bedding, sacks of grain, cracker-boxes and bacon sides were piled up, but this not being sufficient, the bodies of dead horses and mules were dragged to the line and made use of for defence. A pit was sunk in the centre of the square, and in this hole in the ground the surgeon placed his wounded, himself being one of the unfortunates. This, then, was the situation of a command of able-bodied, well-equipped soldiers, strong men every one, which, a few hours previously, had struck its camp and marched in all confidence into this valley of death. Where were now the flaunting guidons and the rude jokes about cowardly redskins? Instead thereof, many were mourning the sudden taking away of beloved comrades, whose bodies were left on the plain to the savage enemy, and all bemoaned the fate of their noble commander, also left on the field. He had proudly led them forward, and when the unlooked-for attack fell upon them still kept at the front; perhaps, having recognised too late the error of over-confidence, he determined to repair the fault even at the sacrifice of his life.

Thornburgh was a noble man, and beloved by all. The troops following him were as good as any in the army, and would have proved more than a match for the enemy if they could have gone into the fight on anything like equal terms.

After dark on this first night a volunteer was called for to take one of the horses yet left alive and if possible steal his way through the enemy's line to the nearest telegraph station. From several volunteers Private Murphy of D Troop, 5th Cavalry, was selected to take this desperate ride, and he accomplished the distance of 170 miles to the railroad in less than 24 hours.

The place selected or rather forced upon Captain Payne, 5th Cavalry, now the senior officer, for the defence of his command, was near the battlefield, and fortunately within reach of the stream called Milk River. It was in a small round valley or opening in the mountains, and within easy rifle range of the tops of the nearest hills surrounding it. On these hills the Indians took position, and while being concealed and well protected themselves, the Indians were able to pick off any soldier showing himself above the breastwork, or while moving about inside of it. The soldiers returned the fire occasionally, but it is not known that an Indian was injured during the siege. The enemy, however, was kept down close behind the ridge, and no advance or open attack on the entrenchment was at any time attempted. The position taken was on a rise or table, and was about two hundred yards from the stream.

No water could be obtained during the day, but after dark a party started out to fill their buckets and canteens. They were almost im-

mediately fired upon by the enemy, who, anticipating their necessities, had found concealment on the further side of the river in the thick underbrush. As some of the party were wounded, they returned to the breastwork unsuccessful. Water being an absolute necessity, even if it cost life, another party was sent out, this time under escort of armed men. As soon as the party was fired upon, the escort discharged their guns, and although firing in the dark and at random, it is supposed that one or more of the enemy were wounded; at any rate the Indians fled, and the troops were not prevented after that from getting water at night sufficient for the next day.

With the dawn of the second day commenced the firing upon the troops from the hill-tops. Not an Indian could be seen on whom to return the fire; only a puff of white smoke indicated from time to time where the bullet came from; and as there was little chance of finding the Indian at the spot from which he had fired, there seemed to be no use wasting ammunition on space, and firing by the troops was kept up only to prevent open attack. On this day nearly all the animals remaining alive were easily disposed of by the enemy, and some men were killed and wounded. Among the latter were Lieutenant Paddock and Surgeon Grimes. The long weary hours of this day must have been trying indeed to the besieged. The suffering and groans of the wounded seemed more terrible than the sight of the bodies of the dead, which could not be removed except at the expense of other lives. It is said that after night these bodies became part of the breast-work, and were used to protect the living.

Exciting accounts have been published of the situation of a party of our countrymen held fast by the ice of the frozen north. It may be said that they had rations, were comparatively comfortable, and had only to wait for a return of the sun to thaw their prison doors and set them free. But these soldiers, although nearer home, were brought to a stand where a life was called for at every crack of the rifle, and where to them the light of day was the season of distress. From the number of lives already lost in this short time, and the number of wounded requiring care and increasing the anxiety, and considering the time that must elapse before help could possibly reach them, an hour here contained more real suffering than could be felt in many days of waiting only for the sun to shine.

Aside from being constantly harassed by the enemy from the outside, an incident occurred on the inside of the works this day that came near finishing the lives of some of the wounded. One of the

165

UTES WATCHING FOR THE RELIEF COLUMN

horses was shot in such a manner as to make him frantic and unmanageable. He charged about the enclosure in a furious way until exhausted, and then fell into the pit among the wounded, fortunately no one was injured, but some of the men said that in their nervous condition they thought the whole Ute nation had jumped from the tops of the hills to the bottom of the pit.

At an early hour on the morning of October 2nd, the sentinel heard the approach of a column of horsemen, and the besieged soon welcomed Captain Dodge, 9th Cavalry, at the head of his troop. The captain, having heard of the situation, came at once to the assistance of his comrades, and managed to get through to the entrenchment without losing any of his men. This reinforcement of two officers and fifty enlisted men added materially to the fighting strength of the command, and they brought with them also the cheering news that the courier had passed through safely. The horses upon which this party rode were soon disposed of by the enemy, and Dodge and his troop became as much of a fixture as any of the besieged. The gallant dash made by these coloured troopers brought them into high favour with the rest of the command, and nothing was considered too good for the "Buffalo" soldiers after that. Captain Dodge almost immediately received well-merited promotion, and was the hero of the campaign.

Leaving the besieged to worry through the days and nights that are to pass before relief can reach them, we will go with the swiftly riding courier, and see what follows his arrival at the railroad.

On the morning of October 1st, our quiet garrison at Fort D, A. Russell, near Cheyenne, Wyoming, was aroused by the information received from Department Headquarters, that Thornburgh and most of his command had been massacred by the Ute Indians, and that the few officers and men remaining were entrenched, protecting the wounded and fighting for their lives. The commanding officer. General Wesley Merritt, fortunately possessing all the characteristics of a true cavalryman, always had his command well in hand. At this time he had four troops of the 5th Cavalry and one company of the 4th Infantry, and when this sudden call reached him all that was necessary was to sound "boots and saddles" and go.

The order to take the field reached us about 8 a. m., and at 11 a. m. we had saddled up, had marched two miles, and were loaded on the cars,—horses, equipments, pack-mules, rations and all,—and were under way. We reached Rawlins Station, our stopping place, about 1 a. m. next morning, and met there four companies of the 4th Infantry, also

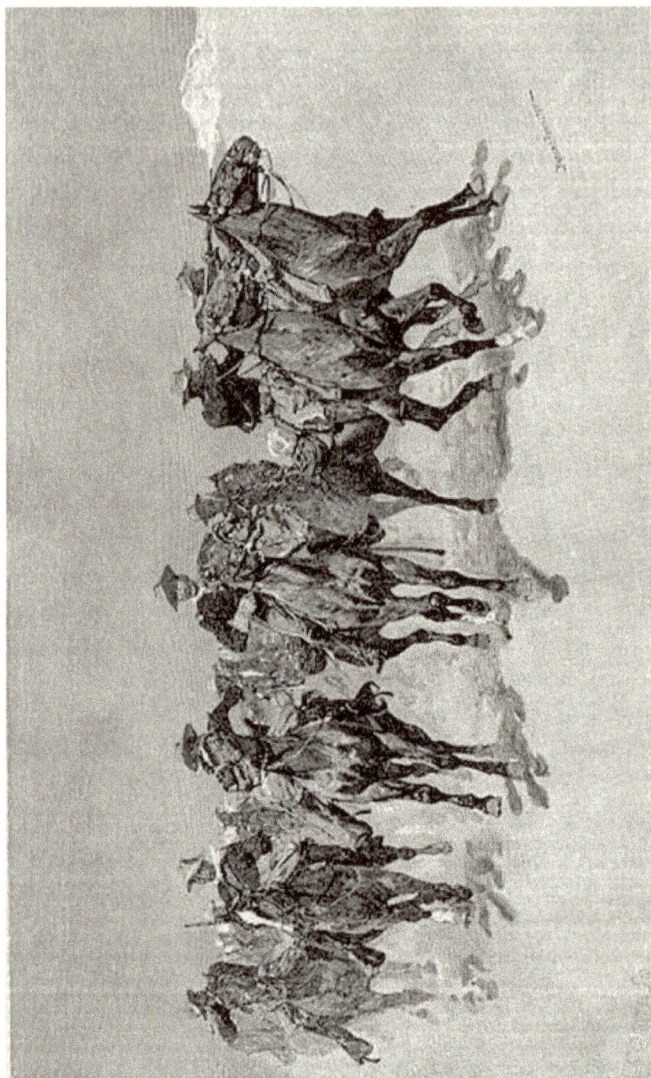

CAPTAIN DODGE'S COLOURED TROOPERS TO THE RESCUE

ordered for field service under General Merritt. The rest of that night was spent in preparing for the march. The infantry, in wagons, were on the road by 10 a. m.; the cavalry marched a little later, but overtook the infantry about twenty-five miles out at 5 p. m. Then all pushed on together until 11 p. m., when it became necessary to halt and rest the animals. At 7 a. m. we were on the road again, and continued marching until 11 p. m., at that time reaching the camp of the infantry company left behind by Major Thornburgh. Here a short rest was taken, and at dawn of day we resumed the march, reaching the entrance to Big Bear Cañon about 4 p. m. This was a rough, ugly looking place to enter with a command at night, especially with the knowledge of disaster in front and not far off.

But the situation called for the greatest exertion, as well as the taking of all the chances, and although we had already made an unheard-of march that day, and on previous days, every man was anxious to go on, and even the animals seemed to be under the influence of the hour. While they were being rubbed down and fed, the men had their coffee and hardtack, and just at dusk we started off for the last march, hoping soon to reach those we knew to be in distress, and who could only be saved by our coming. Getting through that *cañon* at night was a desperate undertaking, leaving the Indians entirely out of the question, and on looking at the breakneck places afterwards by daylight, over which we had passed, it seemed a miracle that we succeeded in getting through without losing all the wagons carrying the infantry, and some of the horsemen as well. The cavalry was in the lead, but the "charioteers," as the infantry were called, followed close behind, and on the down grade occasionally ran into the rear of the cavalry column.

On the ascent the infantrymen jumped from their wagons and pushed horses, wagons and all up the grades. On reaching the summit each party boarded its wagon, and, with a cheer, away they went down the grade on the run. All were under so much of a strain that fatigue or sleep was not thought of. Thus it was, up one hill and down another all night, and no light-artillerymen were ever more expert at mounting their limbers, than these infantrymen in getting out of and into those wagons on the run. Between 4 and 5 a. m. we reached a point about four miles from the entrenchment, and at that hour saw a sight that made the blood run cold. A citizen wagon train, hauling supplies to the agency, had been captured by the Indians, and every man belonging to it had been murdered, stripped, and partly burned.

169

T IDINGS OF THE RELIEF COLUMN—L ISTENING TO THE OFFICERS' CALL

As we had had no news from the front since leaving the railroad, this was something of a surprise, and as may be imagined, at that hour in the morning, not a pleasant opening for the day. The wagon train, for the last few miles, had been stretching out a little, but on reaching this spot it was observed that all intervals were rapidly closed up and kept closed. But notwithstanding this depressing sight, some rude jokes were made, as usual, by the old soldiers in passing, and recruits were made to fear that before another sun should rise they would be broiled in like manner.

General Merritt at this time was some distance ahead with the cavalry, and crossing the last hill he entered the valley just at dawn of day. It was yet too dark to see the entrenchment, but the column, while pressing on, was soon brought to a halt by a challenge from the besieged. A trumpeter was then summoned and officers' call sounded. This brought all hands to the top of the breastwork, and a lively cheer answered the last note on the trumpet. A wild scene followed this coming together of old comrades, and while it was going on, the enemy, although at their posts within easy range, did not fire a shot. Nor did they seem to be alarmed by the arrival of this overpowering force, but were for the time being quiet spectators of this grand reunion, their portion of the fun probably being in the supposition of "more horses, more shoot him."

The general, having the responsibility, was probably the only one of the party in accord with the Indian idea, and consequently, not wasting much time on congratulations, he immediately set to work to prevent the loss of more men or horses.

The rear was safe in the hands of the infantry, and the cavalry was ordered to take the nearest hills on the flanks. This accomplished, the general moved out a short distance to the front, having a troop of cavalry as escort, but did not advance half a mile before being fired upon. We, however, recovered the body of Major Thornburgh, which up to that time had lain upon the battlefield of the first day. Under existing circumstances, a civilized enemy, or such an one as we are taught to fight in text-books and in field manoeuvres, would have made a hasty retreat over the mountains, and any strategist in command could have made certain calculations, but these Ute Indians, instinctively brave and not at all instructed, had the utmost confidence in their power to resist any number of soldiers attacking them in their mountain homes.

The Sioux Indian, on the open plains, likes to show himself as much as possible, thinks to intimidate his foe by such display, and by showing himself at different points in a short space of time, to make several Sioux out of one. On the contrary, the whereabouts of the Ute Indian amongst the rocks of the mountain side, nearly his own colour, cannot easily be discovered; he is not known until the crack of his rifle is heard and his enemy falls, and even then the smoke covers a change of position. It is therefore impossible ever to get a Sioux into the mountains to fight, or to get a Ute out on the plains for the same purpose.

General Merritt, on seeing that the Indians were still determined and prepared to dispute any advance on the part of the soldiers, ordered three troops of cavalry and all the infantry deployed to the front at once. Notwithstanding the fatigue of the long march and no breakfast, the men sprang to their feet and moved forward as if for the first time that day. Quite an exciting skirmish resulted from this advance, and the enemy went dancing round on the hilltops like monkeys, under the short-range fire of the cavalry carbines; but when the infantry battalion, which had deployed behind the crest, came up to the top and opened fire, a change of scene was at once perceptible. The first volley from the infantry rifles made a rolling sound through the mountains like artillery; the Utes ceased the ballet performance and disappeared behind the hill, but still kept up their fire on both infantry and cavalry. The troops, however, adopting the Ute tactics, kept quite as well sheltered, and as it was not the intention to advance further that day, everybody being worn out, the tired soldiers actually went to sleep on the line of battle, a few men being on the lookout and firing occasionally.

About noon there seemed to be some excitement going on among the Indians, and a large white flag was displayed to view. Field-glasses were at once brought to bear, and it was discovered that a white man was waving the flag. Firing on both sides ceased, and the bearer of the flag was allowed to cross the valley and enter our lines. He proved to be an *employé* of the Indian Department, and had been sent up from the Uncumpahgre Agency to stop the war, the White River Utes, with whom we were fighting, being in a way under the control of Colorow, the chief of the Uncumpahgres. It is supposed the Indians were ready to stop anyhow, seeing the amount of force now on the ground and prepared to punish them.

This virtually raised the siege and ended the war. Leaving a light picket line to watch the enemy, the rest of the troops were withdrawn

INFANTRY COVERING THE WITHDRAWAL OF THE CAVALRY

and marched back to the entrenchment, where a jollification was now in order. The wounded were taken out of the loathsome place where they had suffered so many days, and made comfortable. Those who had not been able to wash since the first day's fight now made themselves more presentable and showed their true faces.

The fearful stench from the entrenchment, owing to the material used in its construction, was such as to necessitate a change of camp, and the whole command, accompanied now by the rescued party, moved back on the road about one mile, to clean ground and plenty of pure water.

An unconquerable desire to sleep and rest then overtook these worn-out soldiers. All forms and ceremonies for the rest of that day were dispensed with, and the valley, lately ringing with the sound of men in combat, was now as quiet and still as was its wont.

In this short campaign there were 13 men killed and 48 wounded, out of a command 150 strong.[1] The papers throughout the country mentioned it for a day or two as "the Ute affair," and there it rests, being one of several instances where the percentage of loss is greater than that experienced in battles of which monuments are being erected and elaborate memorials published to commemorate deeds of bravery.

After the command brought down by General Merritt had been well rested and was ready for another advance, it proceeded through the mountains to White River and the agency. It was a beautiful bright morning in October when we bade goodbye to the rescued command under Captain Payne, whose faces were turned towards home, while we marched south to rescue the *employés* at the agency. The infantry and wagon train marched on the road, while the cavalry were well out on the flanks and in advance. The white horses of B Troop, 5th Cavalry, could be seen now and then winding along the crests of the hills on one side, while the blacks of A Troop kept pace with them on the other. No attack could have been made on that column without due warning, and the result was we crossed the high hills and wound through *cañon* after *cañon*, reaching the valley of White River and the agency without hearing a shot or, to my knowledge, seeing an Indian.

At the agency a horrible sight presented itself. Every building had been burned, the bodies of all the male *employés* were stretched upon the ground where they had been murdered a few days before, and the

---

1. Killed 8 & 2 thirds *per cent.*, and 32 *per cent*, wounded.

women had been carried off into a captivity worse than death. After the dead had been buried, the command went into camp on White River. The Indians had taken to the mountains, and in order to follow them it was necessary to abandon wagon transportation and fit up pack trains. While these preparations were going on, we had still another sad experience, and a reminder that the Utes were still near us and relentless enough to take any advantage presenting itself. A party under Lieutenant Hall, regimental quartermaster, was sent out to reconnoitre and look for a trail across the mountains from White River to Grand River.

With this party was Lieutenant William Bayard Weir, of the Ordnance Department, and his sergeant, Humme. Weir went out as a volunteer to accompany Hall, and to hunt. As the party were riding along on the trail, a small herd of deer was discovered off to the left in a ravine. Weir and Humme went after them, while Hall kept on to the front. He had not gone far, however, before he saw fresh Indian signs, and soon afterwards heard sharp firing to his left and rear. On turning back to ascertain the cause and to help Weir if he should be in trouble, he was fired upon himself, and discovered that he was surrounded by Indians. He covered his party as quickly as possible in the dry bed of a stream near at hand, and kept the Indians off until after dark. Then riding into camp he first discovered that Weir had not come in, and reported that he was probably killed.

The battalion of the 5th Cavalry was turned out at once, and, as it was 10 p. m., we had an all-night march ahead of us. Just at dawn we reached the place where Weir had left Hall, and we took his trail and followed it up until we found his dead body lying cold and stiff on the mountain side. This seemed indeed an unnecessary sacrifice. Weir was a noble fellow, beloved by all, and the gathering of that sorrowing crowd of soldiers about his body was a sad experience even to the oldest of them. His face still bore the familiar and kindly expression we knew so well. An overcoat was wrapped around the body, and it was then strapped on a cavalry horse. We returned to camp as sad a funeral procession as one could well imagine.

The country through which we were then operating was a howling wilderness; it is now traversed by railroads and covered with villages and farms. Children at play unwittingly trample the grass over the graves of soldiers who gave their lives that they might live and thrive, and communities throughout the West generally send representatives to Congress, some of whom, in the peace and plenty of their comfortable homes, fail to recognize, in Washington, the hardships, privations, and sacrifice of life suffered by the army, before their prosperity could be possible or the lives of their constituents assured.

In this the simple duty of soldiers was performed, and no credit is claimed, but should not the record of past deeds such as these, accompanied by the prosperity that has followed, at least guarantee a more generous feeling for the army by all citizens, more especially by those who are called upon to support it?

E. V. Sumner,
Lt.-Colonel 5th Cavalry, U. S. A.

The Ute War of 1879

Contents

Why the Indian Bureau Should be Transferred from the Department of the Interior to the Department of War

Our Traditional Policy

When, in 1867, after two years of incessant war, costly beyond precedent among Indian outbreaks in its waste of valuable lives, the main body of hostile Sioux were driven by our cavalry across the British frontiers, our government and people relapsed into that indifference, or rather that absorption in private affairs, which is characteristic of all non-centralized governments and self-governing people, and is peculiarly so of our own.

The volcanic uprising of the Northern States in 1861, was not more national in its character than the indifference with which they had for years regarded the increasing murmurs of war until the cloud no bigger than a man's hand had overspread the sky and the storm had burst. We are too young yet to be far-sighted in our policy; too confident of our ability to apply with crushing force the pound of cure to trouble ourselves to apply through years of comparative quiet the ounce of prevention.

So it is with the Sioux war. The indignation and mourning that overspread the country when Custer's command died in Northern Wyoming, was forgotten when the Sioux were driven across the frontier save in those lonely households where stood a vacant chair. The fever was crushed for the hour what matter it the disease remained. The symptoms are destroyed, never mind the cause. Such has ever been the hand-to-mouth philosophy of our people, and never has it been more strikingly manifest than in our management of the Indians of the Plains.

REVIEW OF THE SIOUX WAR

The pamphlet to which this is an addition, sketches briefly the Sioux war of 1875-77, and makes an urgent plea for the transfer of the Bureau of Indian Affairs from the Interior to the War Department. What were the conditions of the problem then? An Indian tribe was in revolt; the able-bodied warriors had left the agency where at government expense food and clothing were provided for them; settlers were being killed and stock stolen; the frontier towns were in danger. The Indian Bureau, with its machinery of agents, missionaries and contractors, stood helpless. The Indian Sampson had burst the withes of gratitude with which the sentimentalists of the East believed him firmly bound. The sceptre had dropped from the failing hand of the Interior Department when the army stepped on the scene and raised it.

Through weary marches and wakeful nights; through wounds, sickness and death; through summer's heat and winter's snow; against enormous numerical odds led with military skill, and in a country vast, barren and desolate beyond conception; with diminished numbers but undiminished courage and devotion, the little army of the frontier, (a few companies of cavalry and infantry) conquered a peace, vindicated the authority of the government and restored safety. Did we profit by the lesson? Did we institute a system which should make such a revolt impossible and such loss of life unnecessary? I cannot say so. The Interior Department was now equal to the situation. The old method was resumed; the supervision of the army removed; food issued as wastefully and ammunition as prodigally as before the outbreak; murder and theft among the Indians went as before unpunished.

Today, (1879), twenty-five hundred (2,500) warriors of Red Cloud's band lounge about the Sioux agency at Pine Ridge, Nebraska. They are thoroughly armed with long-range rifles, and ammunition purchased from the camp traders under the eye and with the tacit permission of the Interior Department. On the plains around the agency graze twelve thousand (12,000) war ponies, ready for instant service. It is the best mounted, best equipped, and most effective cavalry force of its numbers in the world; and it is a magazine of gunpowder that a spark at any moment may explode.

The slightest cause suffices. Momentary dissatisfaction with the agent; his refusal of some improper demand; even a quarrel among themselves of which he becomes the arbitrator, may scatter these hundreds of savages over the country to kill, burn, and destroy.

History repeats itself. The recent outbreak of the Utes in north-western Colorado has once more called public attention forcibly to the question of Indian management.

What is the position now? A warlike tribe is again in revolt; an agent and his assistant white men murdered and the women of his family brutally ill-treated. United States troops sent to their assistance have been waylaid, attacked, and while withholding their fire have been shot down. The Indian Department again helpless to protect its agents, or to support its theoretically humane policy, has again appealed to the army. With wonderful rapidity it has responded, and now on White River the troops are facing hundreds of armed warriors of this and affiliated tribes. In a word, the Sioux war of '75 is the Ute war of today. The tragedy is acting on the boards of another theatre, the *dramatis personae* are changed, but the argument and the reasoning that applied to the one apply with equal force to the other.

Up to this moment the Indian Bureau has had exclusive control of this tribe. Until the murder of this agent no soldier has set foot within the immense reservation selected for their use. Their love of independence and hatred of restraint has never been crossed by the slightest appearance of armed or forcible authority.

The agents of the Indian Bureau are today with energy, but with little hope, seeking for a cause for this outbreak that shall justify their *protégés* and lay the guilt of this innocent blood elsewhere. Let us also seek for the cause.

The Utes: Numbers and Character

In 1874 the total number of Utes was placed by Gen. Walker, then superintendent of Indian affairs, at 3,800 souls. Of these 3,000 belonged to the Tabequache band, and were located at the Los Pinos agency, in south-western Colorado. Their present chief is Ouray, whose name is now familiar to everyone. As a body they do not appear to have shared in the recent outbreak; but it is probable that a considerable number of their warriors answered the call of their northern brethren, and participated in the attack on Major Thornburgh's command. The remaining 800 of the tribe are divided into three bands: the Yampa, the Grand River and the Uintah, and prominent among their chiefs are Douglass, Johnson and Colorow. The first two bands have an agency on Grand River, in north-western Colorado, and the third band joins them on the west, having a reservation in north eastern Utah.

These three bands are the Indians with whom we have to deal. They are probably somewhat more numerous than in '74. Having been for some years fed, clothed, and blanketed by the government, they have been exempt from the hardships, and loss consequent upon seeking their own subsistence at all seasons, through a rigorous climate and a mountainous country. They have been able to construct comfortable homes near the agency, and under these favourable circumstances have undoubtedly multiplied.

In addition to their own force of matured warriors, say 200, they have drawn to them as many more from the neighbouring tribes with whom they affiliate, and this, with a like contingent from their own people in the south, gives them about 600 to 800 fighting men, which forms the force now facing Gen. Merritt.

The territory occupied by the Utes covers with great exactness the western one-third of the State of Colorado. It is about 300 miles north and south by 150 east and west, and contains 15,000,000 acres, or an average of about 4,000 to each member of the tribe.

Even upon the liberal basis usually employed by the Indian Bureau, this immense territory seemed needless and undesirable for their number, besides greatly in creasing the cost of feeding them, and in '72 negotiations were entered into by the government for their consolidation in the northern part. They were, however, never perfected nor the scheme carried out. The superintendent adds that the Utes "have thus far shown but little interest in the pursuits of civilized life, or the education of their children."

The opinion is generally held and expressed that the Utes have been distinctly and to an unusual degree friendly with the whites. In the abstract sense this is erroneous.

For many years before the pioneers saw Pike's Peak a war of extermination had existed between the Utes and the Sioux. The North Park in Colorado, has been the scene of more than one pitched battle (of which the writer has seen the relics); and it is their inherited hatred (in which fear of a powerful enemy mingles) deeper in an Indian breast than any feeling of antipathy for ourselves, together with their isolated position on the western slope of the Rocky Mountains, that has prevented serious breaches between them and the whites.

But though extensive outbreaks have been infrequent, incursions beyond their reservation (large as it is) have been the rule rather than the exception; and many a hunter and ranchman in the North and Middle Parks, fifty miles beyond reservation limits, has been murdered during the past ten years; his stock stolen, his ranch burned and his property destroyed. A dozen such in stances have occurred this summer, the details of which can be cited if necessary.

Having thus stated the general conditions surrounding these Indians, let us consider briefly the events of the last four months.

THE MURDERS AT THE AGENCY

For a year past, and at the date of their outbreak, the U. S. Indian Agent for the White River Utes was N. C. Meeker. Mr. Meeker was for many years the trusted friend of Horace Greeley and assistant editor of the N. Y. *Tribune*. In 1869 he headed the colony that built the town of Greeley, Colorado. For several years he resided there, and edited the Greeley *Tribune*, and by his counsels and character greatly added to the prosperity of the town. Liberal, unprejudiced, humane, and filled with the best type of Christian philosophy, Meeker earnestly believed that the Indian of the plains could be civilized by kindness, elevated by education and made self-supporting by example and precept. He was fully in accord with the views of the highest eastern philanthropists on the question of Indian management, and was selected by the Indian Bureau for that reason.

He went to his post prepared to execute in letter and in spirit the instructions he had received. He accepted the position not more for personal benefit than to prove the truth of the theory in which he believed. He fought the good fight, and he testified to his fidelity with his life. He was the highest and purest type of Indian agent. Under no one could the principle of appeal to the higher nature of the Indian have been more fully, faithfully and persistently tried. He proved by the circumstances of his death the falsity, the hopelessness, the criminal folly, of such treatment, unassisted and unprotected by armed force, being applied to the inherently treacherous, cruel and brutal character of the warlike Indians of the "plains." He died because the higher nature to which he would have appealed, the feeling of gratitude, of honour, of good faith, of respect for promises (saving in some exceptional cases) *does not exist*.

Let us briefly sketch the painful story:

In the spring of this year Mr. Meeker, following the instructions of his Department, set his white assistants to plough the land about the agency buildings; endeavoured to get the adult male Indians to aid in the work; and gathered the children, so far as possible, into a daily school. The sick of all ages he and his family personally nursed and attended.

From the outset the work and schooling were violently opposed by the Indians, their repeated complaints being that no more ploughing should be done and no school kept.

Note the complaint. Not lack of provisions; not ill-treatment from a tyrannical or dishonest agent; not the infringements of miners, for none were nearer than Hahn's Peak, a hundred miles away; not the threatened loss of their lands or hunting, for there are no settlers nearer at any time than Bear River, fifty miles from the reserve; not the presence of soldiers, for none were at any time located nearer than two hundred miles; but unqualified refusal that their lands, for *their* benefit, should be ploughed, or their children taught.

They met the issue boldly and at once. To feed and be clothed in idleness, at government expense, they were willing; but the first step towards making them self-supporting they determined to meet with war.

Nothing at any time did they say about "Father" Meeker, but that he urged on them the benefits of civilization, and yet, when their plans were matured, they killed him without compunction, and without the most trivial pretext.

And here it is proper to say that the mining discoveries in the North Park of Colorado, which are the only ones that approximate the White River Utes, and which have been so often cited by the newspapers as an encroachment on Indian boundaries and a pregnant cause of trouble, do not at any point approach the reservation nearer than one hundred miles. The charge is so plausible and so readily believed at the East, that in spite of its frequent refutation, it constitutes a staple part of the Indian apologist's stock in trade.

Events culminated in July of this year. Mr. Meeker, already an old man, was violently beaten and dangerously injured by a Ute chief named Johnson, whom he had greatly befriended, and who had frequently eaten at his table. The white labourers were fired on and driven to seek refuge in the agency buildings.

Col. Jno. W. Steele, of Kansas City, who visited the agency at that time on private business, found him at his home, propped up in his chair and suffering severely. To him Meeker made the following statement, which speaks more eloquently than can any words of mine:

I came to this agency in the full belief that I could civilize these Utes. That I could teach them to work and become self-supporting. I thought that I could establish schools and interest both Indians and their children in learning. I have given my best efforts to this end, always treating them kindly, but firmly. They have eaten at my table, and received continued kindness from my wife and daughter, and all the *employés* about the agency. Their complaints have been heard patiently, and all reasonable requests have been granted them, and now, the man for whom I have done the most, for whom I have built the only Indian house on the reservation, and who has frequently eaten at my table, has turned on me without the slightest provocation, and would have killed me but for the white labourers who got me away. No Indian raised his hand to prevent the outrage, and those who had received continued kindness from myself and family, stood around and laughed at the brutal assault. They are an unreliable and treacherous race.

To this he added that the whole complaint of the Indian was against the ploughing and the school; that Douglass, the head chief of this agency, had no followers and but little influence, and that the larger part of the tribe, under the lesser chiefs, Colorow, Jack and Johnson, had been away from the reservation all summer against his protest and orders. We now know that these absent Indians had been two hundred miles from their reserve; had killed white men in the North Park and on Bear and Snake Rivers, and destroyed their cattle and buildings, and had burned the timber and grass over immense tracts of country.

With Indian sagacity, and evidently in pursuance of well matured plans, they early in the summer burned all the grass over which cavalry must pass from the Union Pacific Railroad to the agency. On every hand they traded their stock of furs and hides for rifles and ammunition of the best quality. Within six weeks from the outbreak the trader at the agency sold to them three cases of Winchester rifles and a large amount of ammunition, and from the unscrupulous whites, camped about the border of the reserve, they obtained further large supplies of both. Gen. Merritt on his arrival with the troops after Meeker's murder, apprehended a number of these men, and from one alone seized 12,000 rounds of cartridge.

The situation grew more threatening, and on September 10th, and not till then, the brave old agent asked for troops to save the white lives at the agency.

Major Thornburgh with a small command started at once from Fort Fred Steele, on the Union Pacific Railroad, but before aid could reach them the blow had fallen. When, after many days, the first troops reached the agency, they found the buildings burnt, and the dead bodies of every white man, including Meeker, who had been employed there. The bodies were stripped naked and mutilated in Indian fashion.

No more causeless or deliberate murder; no stronger illustration of the savage instinct when unrestrained can be found in our Indian annals.

Hostilities Begun by the Indians—Apologies for them by Agents of the Indian Bureau

An effort has been widely made by the Department of the Interior, both through its chief clerks at Washington and its special and permanent agents in Colorado, (seconded by such papers as the New York *Times*) to convince the public that the Indians throughout this struggle have acted on the defensive only; have deprecated violence; have precipitated no encounter, and have been the attacked and not the attacking party. To refute this wholly untrue and malicious statement it is worth while to review the Thornburgh engagement; but while we do so it will be impossible for the fair-minded observer to repress a feeling of indignation that the department that had called upon the army for assistance in a moment of great peril, induced by its own folly, and been promptly answered, should permit its agent to publicly charge upon the men then risking their lives for it, the provocation and prolongation of the difficulty.

Was Major Thornburgh, or were the Utes the attacking party?

Setting aside the murders, thefts and depredations of the Indians during the summer beyond their reserve; this burning of grass and other preparations to isolate the agency from the aid of troops; the gathering of warriors from adjacent tribes; their purchase and careful accumulation of arms; ignoring the murder of Meeker and his *employés*, for which absolutely no cause is alleged by their Washington apologists, (evidence hardly admitting of argument to an impartial mind) let us see whether they wanted peace or war when they first came face to face with United States troops.

Entering the mouth of the canyon, through which runs the little stream of Milk Creek, the skirmishers of Thornburgh's advance discovered a heavy ambuscade. The troops were stopped and a lieutenant advanced with a few men. He went forward waving a white hand-kerchief and giving every sign of a desire to communicate, and was received with a shower of bullets, the Indians shouting, in plain English, curses and the most abusive epithets! Had such an action come from the troops what would have been the comments of the Eastern press? Could language strong enough have been found by the Interior Department to express its horror?

Making no return fire, the officer fell back to the advance where was Thornburgh in person. By a rapid movement on their flanks, a large number of Indians threw themselves between the advance and the main body, pouring in a sharp fire. Having withheld his men from firing up to this moment, under a conscientious and al most suicidal observance of the spirit of his orders, Thornburgh then ordered a charge and fell gallantly in leading it. Gentlemen of the Interior Department! You will hardly wish to put over your own names a charge that this engagement was "provoked by the army." The five days siege that followed, the suffering of the gallant little command in their rifle pits, the magnificent march, rarely equalled in military annals, of Gen. Merritt's troops to their relief, and the rescue that followed are matters of history.

To one more incident of the campaign I wish to allude: On the twentieth of October two officers, one of them Lieut. Weir, were sent with six scouts from the camp of Gen. Merritt's command on White River, to discover a reported wagon road through the mountains to the south. After riding some hours, Lieut. Weir and one scout separated slightly from the others to explore a ravine. Very quickly the report of rifles reached the larger party. Attempting to return, they were fired on by a body of mounted Indians much larger than their own, and with difficulty defended themselves till dark. They reached the main camp at midnight, returned with reinforcements and found the body of Lieut. Weir within a half mile of the point where he left the command, and that of the scout not far from it.

Gen. Adams, Special Commissioner of the Interior Department, has made this event the subject of a report that has been widely published, and for what end? To perpetuate the memory of the gallant officer, or to record a regret that such a noble life had been lost, for it would have been impossible to find one of greater promise? Not at all. That is not the mission of the agents of the Indian Bureau. He alludes to this event, which has carried mourning to hundreds of hearts over the land, only that he may apologize for the murderers! Only that he may lay before the public an excuse for their act! He tells us *on the authority of the Indians* that they did not fire until first attacked. Let us calmly consider it.

Lieut. Weir was shot and died instantly. He had left the command but a few moments. The Indians who killed him numbered a score. Within half an hour afterward they waylaid the remainder of the party and made the attack—suddenly and with desperation, firing first, and keeping them surrounded for hours They were fresh from the surprise and attempted massacre of Thornburgh's command; fresh from the murder of the gray haired Meeker and his assistants.

Shall we accept as truth such a statement? A statement without shadow of probability, and to which all experience gives the lie? Or, had Lieut. Weir and his scout, suddenly surrounded by an ambuscade of savages, been fortunate enough to fire first, would not every sane man have applauded the action? Had any white man reason to expect his life from men who had within a week murdered the old and defenceless, and had strewn the country far and wide with the corpses of white men?

I am certain of the verdict of my countrymen, which ever was the case. It will remember with reverence the memory of Weir and record his death as occurring in self-defence while in the execution of a duty; and it will brand with indignation and with contempt the motives and character of the man who could make himself the mouthpiece for such an apology.

In touching at length upon the details of this Ute war I have had a special object. First: To show that no infringement of rights or failure to fulfil treaty obligations had taken place. Second: To prove that the Indians have in every way assumed the initiative.

For many of our former Indian wars some distinct cause or series of causes can be assigned; some wrong or fancied wrong sustained by the tribe, sometimes trifling, occasionally serious. In this instance the historian will seek in vain. It can be characterized only as the natural and infallible result of abandoning the use of force (humanely exercised but still force, positive and irresistible) as a means of Indian government and substituting for it the Golden Rule. The natural result of an attempt to change the lives and control the habits of a totally savage and warlike people, relying for your coercive machinery on Christian maxims and rations of bread and beef.

CHARACTER OF THE INDIAN AGENTS. TREATMENT OF
MR. MEEKER'S FAMILY

Of the various Indian agents whose dispatches, monotonous in tone, fill the papers, I have a word to say. Stanley and others inform us daily that "everything is quiet." They did so when hundreds of Indians were pouring a ceaseless fire into Thornburgh's rifle pits, and when the shots that killed Weir and his scout were ringing through the woods.

They are exponents of the "policy." They are struggling to hold their positions and salaries. The truth is the last thing they seek, and one can almost smile at their chagrin as their turbulent and savage *protégés* daily give the lie to the agent's carefully prepared dispatches.

Of the many fraudulent combinations for robbing the government during the last twenty years, it is probable that none has gained wider or more unenviable notoriety than the Indian Ring. The amount of money handled yearly in contracts has been immense, the peculation enormous and the profits proportionate. Men of large means, and well known in Washington and the East, have been concerned in it, and from this source has come the desperate, and only really effective, opposition to the transfer of the Indian Bureau to the war office.

Every effort to this end has been persistently contested by the Ring in its passage through the Houses, in the appointment of the committee, and among the committee after entering on its duties. The immense profits realised have furnished the "sinews of war," and success has thus far followed the judicious use of the large sums at their command. As details give, oftentimes, reality to a picture, I will say here, that a member of the Congressional committee that visited the west in 1878, to investigate the wisdom of the proposed transfer, stated openly in Cheyenne, that before leaving Washington he had been offered thirty thousand dollars to make an adverse report.

It is not perhaps entirely irrelevant to add that the majority report of the committee *was adverse.*

To Commissioner Adams we wish to do exact justice. At considerable danger he penetrated to the hostile camp, and obtained possession of the captive white women. For the relief that the country felt that their lives were spared let him have full credit. But when he gives us to understand that they had been treated with kindness, and their persons respected, he states for the benefit of his department, and his employers, a deliberate untruth.

The ladies were robbed, stripped and beaten by Indians whom

they had personally nursed in sickness, and fed at their table. Mrs. Meeker was carried half fainting on a mule for sixty miles, without rest, and from sheer barbarity without a saddle; and the Chief Douglass, their protector, according to Commissioner Adams, held a cocked and loaded rifle to the heads of the others while endeavouring to make them yield to his brutal lusts.

That I may not be accused of having set down "aught in malice" I here append a further *verbatim* statement of two of the ladies, made in Denver on their arrival. How much remains unstated can be only surmised:

"What do you think of Douglass, Mrs. Meeker, and how has he used you?"

"He has treated me dreadfully. It seems to me sometimes that he was trying to see how much torture I could bear without dying. He is the worst one of these Utes. Jack is a brave warrior, but Douglass is cunning and treacherous. If any of them ought to be punished he is the one."

The reporter turned to Mrs. Price and said:

"Mrs. Price, Douglass says he had nothing to do with the massacre at the agency, that Jack's band did it. Is that true?"

"No, he was the man that started it all. Jack's band fought the soldiers, and Douglass and his men killed the *employés*. I saw him during the fight with a gun in his hand, swearing and drunk. All of the Indians were drunk that night; they took all the medical supply whiskey, and besides they had some they got from ranchmen on the reservation. While Douglass was drunk he told me a lot of things that he don't know of now. If he had remembered he would have killed me. He arranged the whole thing, and the soldiers coming has made him afraid, and he is trying to get out of it now. He's the smartest and meanest of them all."

Position of the Army toward the Interior Department

It is well here to point out the falsity of the position in which the Department of War and the Department of the Interior stand toward each other.

The Department of the Interior undertakes the government of 300,000 savages, scattered from Mexico to British America, and from the Mississippi River to the Pacific Ocean; of characters as various as the climate in which they live. It undertakes to suppress and punish crime; to stop raids on the settlements and on neighbouring Indians;

to confine the tribes to certain limits; to feed, clothe, educate and civilize. It purposes doing this through its machinery of civil agents, unsupported by any assistance from the army. Annually, monthly, this scheme fails in some part of the west, and the army are called on to save life. The troops scattered over a thousand miles square, of territory, are hurried to the spot as rapidly as steam and horse flesh can compass the distance. The cost is enormous. The first detachment arrives, is met by overpowering numbers, and perhaps repulsed, losing valuable lives. When the Indians find themselves over matched they retire. The old chiefs communicate with the agents of the Indian Bureau, and deny responsibility. The army is checked; is held for weeks inactive in camp, losing all advantage gained by rapidity of movement and the surprised condition of the Indians.

Such is the present state of affairs on White River. One of two results must follow: Either a peace, dishonourable to the government, (and now greatly desired by the Indians) will be effected; or Merritt will be ordered to advance, only again to be stopped midway by the Interior Department; remote from supplies, and surrounded by snow, whenever the Indians find themselves in danger of being driven to the wall.

To sum up the situation the army is used as a police force by the Interior Department. It is degraded from its position and deprived of its effectiveness by rarely being allowed to originate or complete a movement, The Secretary of War is shorn of his authority as direc-tor of the army, and our generals become mere chiefs of police under the orders of the Secretary of the Interior. They are expected, with a skeleton of an army, to quell at a moment's notice any insurrection in our enormous territory, and are debarred from taking the practical precau tions that would render such insurrections impossible. Under the present system they are compelled to see the accumulation by the Indians, during the intervals of peace, of all the engines of war, which must render their subjugation enormously difficult when the inevita-ble outbreak comes.

Why the Utes Now Wish For Peace

In considering the general aspect of the Ute question today one phase demands especial attention. It is one universally misunderstood at the East, and which clearly explained, should influence the opin-ion of every sincere man as to the policy to be pursued toward the Indians.

The position and theory of the Indian Bureau is this: That the Indians have acted hastily, are sorry for it, now wish for peace, and as an earnest have restored the women of Meeker's family.

How far the "hasty" action of men who had been accumulating cartridges for months, had burned the ranges and gathered recruits from various tribes to prevent the approach of troops, should be held an excuse for murder, is perhaps not worth argument. Their "sorrow" need hardly excite our sympathy. Their restoration of the women, (though in pitiable condition) does indicate a faltering purpose. They undoubtedly desire a present peace. Why? *Because they are afraid to go to war at the beginning of winter.*

They failed in their grand *coup*, the destruction of Thornburgh, as the Sioux annihilated Custer. They find themselves confronted by Gen. Merritt, with a rapidity and amount of troops of which they had not dreamed: and against which they dare not make a winter campaign. Though tireless and unapproachable in the saddle during summer, when the grass fails they are helpless. Without grain their ponies become too weak to travel, and die. Left on foot among the snowy mountains, with no means of carrying stores of food, *tepees* for shelter, or robes for covering; exposed to a climate unequalled in the United States for severity, the end would be speedy, even were nature alone against them. But they know by experience that they have far more to dread from the troops in winter than in summer.

With grain for their horses, heavy wagon trains for transportation, and warmly clothed, our men have repeatedly shown their ability to keep the field and do effective service through the coldest months. Gen. Crook's winter campaigns, against the Snakes in Idaho, against the Sioux under Crazy Horse, on the Rosebud, and against the Cheyennes at Slim Buttes, have been noted for their success.

For this reason and no other, therefore, do the White River Utes wish for peace. A campaign begun now against them by such a force as Gen. Merritt's would be fatal to them. Driven from one resting place to another through the winter months; their young and old, their sick and wounded dying from exposure, the spring would find their numbers decimated and their power broken. Not realising the number of troops that could in a few days be concentrated against them, the young warriors have been permitted to inaugurate war. Now, seeing that a disastrous pursuit and defeat await them, and that the doors of the agency with its stores of welcome provisions are closed, the Utes undoubtedly "want peace" (for the winter), and any concessions in their power that will accomplish this object they will make.

It is puerile to expect that any considerable number of the men who attacked Thornburgh and murdered Meeker, will be surrendered to justice; there is no power sufficient in Ouray and his followers to arrest or deliver them; and it. is for us to say, whether, under these circumstances, terms of peace shall be accepted; and if so, whether they shall be such as weakly condone the out rages committed, or such as shall vindicate the dignity and authority of the government.

What We Ask of Congress

For relief from this sadly mistaken policy, the people not of the frontier alone, but of the whole country look to the coming Congress. Every town in every county, every county in every state, has its sons in the army that is thus needlessly sacrificed. Congress can furnish this relief in one way only, namely: by a complete and entire transfer of the care of the Indians to the Department of War.

The reasons for such a measure are stated at length in the accompanying pamphlet, and I will not recapitulate.

The events of the past four months form a plea for that transfer, written in letters of blood, and stronger far than any language that I can employ. In the name of Meeker and his family; in the name of the hundreds of gallant soldiers whose lives have been sacrificed in the suppression of Indian outbreaks, during the ten years that have passed since Fetterman and his eighty men were murdered in northern Wyoming; in the name of the hundreds of settlers who today fill unknown graves near the homesteads they cultivated; we demand that the management of the Indians shall be taken from the theorizing and ignorant civilian and given to the practical and experienced soldier. Taken from the men, who under the aegis of the Indian Bureau, have fattened for years on unrighteous contracts, and given to the officers who by character and self interest are removed from such temptations. In a word, taken from the advocates of a "policy," humane in theory but worthless in practice, a policy that has proved a very god Moloch in its destruction of noble lives, and whose failure has been for years written in mourning by many a fireside, and given to men who have no "policy" to advocate, but the straight forward duty to perform of governing the Indians at the least cost of human life.

Thomas Sturgis.

Cheyenne, Wyoming Territory,
Nov. 10th, 1879.

Leonaur Editors' Note

All of the works that compose the contents of this book were written and published very shortly after the events they describe took place. Readers might reasonably require to know the events of the aftermath of the White River Ute War of 1879. Simply put, by 1880, Ouray was dead. All the Utes—those who had risen in rebellion and those who had remained peaceable—were removed to Utah. In 1882 White River Utes led by Jack attempted to return to Colorado. He was killed by government troops and his followers returned to the Utah reservation.

www.ingramcontent.com/pod-product-compliance
Lightning Source LLC
Chambersburg PA
CBHW021057090426
42738CB00006B/375